Grants in the Humanities

A Scholar's Guide to Funding Sources

Grants in the Humanities

A Scholar's Guide to Funding Sources

By William E. Coleman

Neal-Schuman Publishers, Inc.

Published by Neal-Schuman Publishers, Inc.
64 University Place
New York, New York 10003

Published outside North America by Mansell Publishing, 3 Bloomsbury
Place, London WC14 2QA, England.

Printed and bound in the United States of America.

Library of Congress Cataloging in Publication Data

Coleman, William Emmet, 1942-
  Grants in the humanities.

  Includes bibliographies and indexes.
  1. Humanities—Research grants—United States—
Directories.   2.   Research grants—United States—
Directories.   3.   Humanities—Research grants—United
States.   4.   Research grants—United States.   I.   Title.
AZ507.C58   001.4′4   79-25697
ISBN 0-918212-21-9

British Library Cataloguing in Publication Data

Coleman, William E
  Grants in the humanities.
  1. Humanities—Research grants—North America
  —Directories
  2. Humanities—Research grants—North America
  I. Title
  001.3′07′207   AS911.A2

  ISBN 0-7201-1568-X

Contents

Foreword

Scholarship and the arts have always required patronage beyond the resources derived from the sale of their products. The processes of reflection and creation demand long gestation periods in order to reach their full flowering. Whether the end result is a symphony, a new theory of knowledge, a statue, a novel, a painting, or a history of a past civilization, it exists as the accumulated distillation of its maker's talent and learning, shaped through work over time with no reliable assurance of the final product's quality and impact. In this sense, art and scholarship always involve a calculated risk, for the individual practitioner and for society as well.

Every society has devised mechanisms to balance the inherent uncertainties of this process, enabling some of its most gifted members to devote themselves to study and to the creative arts. In many past ages such support was given on an individual, idiosyncratic basis by the noble or wealthy, to the few lucky individuals who chanced to please a patron. Governments too have contributed their share of support, though often through the strong interest of one person—the ruler or a member of his or her close circle.

In western society the Catholic Church served as an institutional patron of the arts and scholarship for centuries, decorating its sanctuaries with architectural design, painting, and sculpture; commissioning musical works for its rituals and giving employment to thousands of musicians of every kind; fostering scholarship in its monasteries at the same time as it preserved manuscripts, documents, and books which would form the intellectual heritage of future generations.

Because the United States was founded on democratic principles and lacked a noble class or state-endorsed religious hierarchy, the question of support for scholars and artists was thrown open in a completely novel way, which demanded new responses. Ultimately, private wealth assumed the pathfinder's role, first through individual and then institutionalized philanthropy. The private foundation as we know it was essentially an American invention. For at least 50 years, foundations sustained the advancement of knowledge in America in many fields, in the absence of systematic support from governmental sources.

The success of this experiment has been unprecedented. The number of foundations in the United States is large, even now in a period when stringent tax laws and spiralling inflation have caused some private foundations to reduce their scale of operations or close. The *Foundation Directory* lists 3,138 foundations in its most recent edition (1979). Of these, 545 are company-sponsored, 81 are community foundations, and 3,012 are independent private foundations, including both operating and nonoperating foundations. About one-third of these are regional or national in their giving; the others are predominantly local.

These 3,138 foundations own about 90 percent of all foundation assets in this country. The remaining 10 percent are possessed by an additional 23,000 smaller foundations, not included in the Directory. In 1978, these foundations distributed $2,007,159,775 in grants. The average grant size was $6,653. Approximately 27 percent of this went to education and another 10 percent to the humanities ($153,400,000).

Surprisingly, although the Tax Reform Act of 1969 somewhat inhibits the formation of new foundations, more than 5 percent of all foundations in the Directory's seventh edition have been created in the 1970s. Twenty of these are foundations with substantial assets, totalling $16 million or more. Thirty are company foundations, 132 are independent foundations. This represents a very encouraging trend which could not have been predicted in the early 1970s, when it appeared that the effects of the Tax Reform Act might well be to reduce the total number of existing foundations and restrict the formation of new ones.

To the resources provided by Foundation support, the last fifteen years have added welcome growth in governmental agencies which nourish the arts and humanities. Though established much later than equivalent agencies for scientific research, the National Endowments for the Arts and the Humanities have grown into a secure public base for assistance to the creators and thinkers in our society.

Grants in the Humanities by William Coleman is a testimony to the wealth of our national experiment in evolving diverse ways to fund humanistic research, thought, and writing. Perhaps the most significant weakness in the chain of information and monetary assistance for American scholars in the humanities is the one this book seeks to remedy: the need for easily accessible information on where sources of support exist, what areas they fund, and how they should be approached. Natural and social scientists have been notably enterprising and assertive in locating funding sources, in creating informal information networks among themselves about where and how grants may be obtained, and in publicizing such opportunities formally. Until now, humanists have suffered from a scarcity of both formal and informal guideposts. Humanists tend to engage less frequently in collective research, and do not have the scientists' compelling need for costly research implements and laboratories. Perhaps, therefore, their environment may have been less naturally conducive to the sharing of information, as well as providing fewer inescapable financial pressures which would impell them to outside sources of support. It may have seemed less essential to spend time and energy tracking down funding sources when that effort could more easily go into one's own work instead.

In today's economic climate, however, it is no longer easy simply to forego the quest for outside funding. Universities are reducing their internal reinforcement for scholarship in response to their own economic pressures, by making fewer faculty grants available and placing more restrictions on leave time for research. At the same time, publication is becoming even more critical to career advancement than it was formerly.

In November 1973, the Mediaeval Academy of America held a meeting of its members, hosted by the Dumbarton Oaks Center for Byzantine Studies in Washington, D.C. The conferees were much concerned about "pure research" fields in the humanities—disciplines such as their own which explore a historic period and advance our understanding of its life and experience, without necessarily uncovering any knowledge directly applicable in contemporary terms. In fact, it happens often that a scholarly discovery from research of this kind does have implications that are of real value to us today, but as is the case in "pure" scientific research, the outcome cannot be predicted before the project is completed. On the last afternoon of the conference, several of us stood on the terrace overlooking the formal gardens of Dumbarton Oaks in the brilliant blue and gold autumn sunshine and probed the ways in which information on funding could best be collected and made available to the Academy's members.

It is to William Coleman's credit that he did not forget. Like a knight in a medieval romance gathering up a gauntlet flung in challenge, he picked up the project thrown at him by his colleagues that afternoon and out of that task has assembled a guide useful not just for medievalists, but for humanists of every discipline and period of study. I believe he has performed a fine service: for humanists who seek to increase our store of knowledge, and for those of us who work in foundations and wish to make more widely available the information which applicants need. We can all be grateful for the result.

D. Lydia Brontë
Program Officer,
    Central Administration
The Rockefeller Foundation

Preface

This project originated at a meeting of the Centers and Regional Associations (CARA) group of the Mediaeval Academy of America which took place at Dumbarton Oaks, Washington, D.C., in November 1973. One of the themes of the meeting was the importance of gaining grant support for medieval research. At the end of the conference, I volunteered to prepare a guide to grant moneys available to medievalists.

The original plan was for a short list of the major foundations that have supported research of interest to the members of the Mediaeval Academy. But in organizing this list I realized that the business of grantsmanship is so extraordinarily complex that a rather longer and more detailed report would better serve the needs of medievalists searching for funds to support their research.

It also became apparent that the scope of the list would have to be expanded. The range of areas that are the subject of medieval research is extraordinary—fields as varied as languages, literature, law, and history, science, art and anthropology. I was, in other words, dealing with a variety of subjects as broad as that described in the definition of the humanities which is used by the National Endowment for the Humanities.[1] But despite this great variety, very few foundation grants, scholarships, or fellowships are reserved specifically for medieval research. The best solution to the problem, then, was to construct a general guide to support for study and research in the humanities. When the guide was finally completed, it had grown to a size much larger than the modest finding list which had originally been envisioned. Since then, it has been even further revised and expanded.

Grants in the Humanities has been written for the more than 200,000 American scholars and teachers (as well as for foreign scholars and teachers) with advanced degrees in the humanities. Although they constitute about 18 percent of the full and part-time faculty at American colleges and universities, humanists have heretofore never had a book such as this designed specifically for their needs. Most of the moneys awarded to individuals each year go to scientists and to social scientists. Furthermore, most of the publications in the field of grantsmanship have been directed toward the sciences. As a result, humanists have had to make do largely with the general guides to funding and grantsmanship that have already been published. (These are listed in an annotated bibliography that follows Chapter One.) Many humanists teach at colleges and universities that employ a grants officer, but these often harried grants officers do not have the time to invest in guiding humanities grant proposals, which tend to have budgets of less than $10,000, through the application process. As a matter of practicality, grants officers spend the majority of their time attending to the science proposals, with their generally much larger budgets. So *Grants in the Humanities* has been designed for the reference section of the college library, for the individual humanist, and for the college grants officer's bookshelf.

The prime concern of *Grants in the Humanities* is postdoctoral research. Information about scholarships and fellowships for graduate work in the humanities is available in a variety of publications.[2] Likewise, information about medals, honors, and prizes has already been published.[3] The guide does, however, list several scholarships for which graduate students working on the dissertation and younger postgraduates are eligible. Another qualification is that the guide lists only those funding agencies which do not limit themselves to residents of a particular geographical area. But the report does describe the work of the Foundation Center, which provides the means to identify these smaller and local granting agencies. Finally, this guide has been prepared for individuals. It is not concerned with foundations that only support institutions or provide educational development grants. The seeking of these institutional grants is a different process—one best managed by a professional grants officer.

Grants in the Humanities deals with the world of foundations and grants in four chapters: the first discusses the means by which scholars can identify grant sources for their research and some suggestions about preliminary contacts with a foundation; the second chapter describes the process of preparing and submitting a grant proposal, including how to organize the grant proposal, with ideas on budget preparation. This is followed by a chapter where a sample proposal and budget are discussed. The fourth chapter is a discussion of the successful grant applicant's income tax, as well as what to do when one's grant proposal is turned down.

Five appendixes follow. The first lists those agencies with a primary interest in providing grant support to individuals doing research in the humanities. It is the largest section of the report, for it contains the name, address, and vital information of over 130 agencies. This information has been thoroughly cross-indexed at the end of the book. Appendix B is a calendar of deadlines for the grant programs in Appendix A. Appendix C describes the services of the Federal Information Centers. Appendix D describes the work of the Foundation Center, with its four national collections and 76 cooperating collections. Finally, Appendix E lists state humanities committees which fund local humanities projects.

There are also two indexes to the volume. The subject index lists, by subject, agencies granting money for research or study in a particular area of the humanities. The geographic index is an alphabetical listing of places in the world where the scholar can go to do research. Both indexes are keyed to the agencies listed in Appendix A.

Because of the accelerating rate of change in humanities grant programs during the past several years, many granting agencies have been frequently modifying their programs. The publishers and I hope therefore that *Grants in the Humanities* will be revised for annual publication.

Several people have aided the completion of *Grants in the Humanities.* I would like to thank Elizabeth Walldov, Supervisor of Grant Coordination at the Research Foundation of the City University of New York, for her advice on proposal design and budget construction. D. Lydia Brontë, Program Officer, Central Administration, at the Rockefeller Foundation, encouraged this project when it was first suggested at Dumbarton Oaks in 1973 and graciously accepted my invitation to write the foreword to this book. Ira Bloomgarden, former Chairman of the English Department at John Jay College, arranged for partial released time when I was doing the preliminary research for the project. Portia Edwards did a splendid job of typing the manuscript. Finally, my wife, Edvige Agostinelli Coleman has been a constant source of encouragement and support during the writing of this book.

William E. Coleman
Department of English/Thematic Studies
John Jay College of Criminal Justice
City University of New York

NOTES:

1. The National Foundation on the Arts and the Humanities Act of 1965 defines the term "humanities" to include the study of the following: "language, both modern and classical; linguistics; literature; history; jurisprudence; philosophy; archeology; the history, criticism, theory and practice of the arts; and those aspects of the social sciences which have humanistic content and employ humanistic methods." In 1970, Congress added ethics and comparative religion to the fields supported by the Endowment. More recently, the following has been added: "the study

and application of the humanities to the human environment with particular attention to the relevance of the humanities to the current conditions of national life."

2. *Annual Register of Grant Support* (Chicago: Marquis Academic Media, annual); *Awards for Graduate Study and Research*. Statistics Canada: Education, Science, and Culture (Ottawa: Information Canada, 1973); *Barron's Educational Series* (Great Neck, New York: Barron's, as follows: *Barron's Compact Guide to Colleges*. rev. ed. 1978; Nicholas C. Proia and Vincent M. DiGaspari, *Barron's Handbook of American College Financial Aid*. rev. ed. 1978; Samuel C. Brownstein and Mitchel Weiner, *Barron's How to Prepare for College Entrance Examinations*. rev. ed. 1978); *Catalogue of Federal Education Assistance Programs: An Indexed Guide to the Federal Government's Programs Offering Educational Benefits to the American People* (Washington, D.C.: Department of Health, Education, and Welfare, 1974); *Grants for Graduate Study Abroad* (New York: Institute of International Education, annual); Robert Quick, ed. *A Guide to Graduate Study: Programs Leading to the Ph.D. Degree*. 4th ed. (Washington, D.C.: American Council on Education, 1969); *Lovejoy's College Guide*. 13th ed. (New York: Simon & Schuster, 1976); S. Norman Feingold and Marie Feingold, *Scholarships, Fellowships, and Loans*. vol. 6 (Arlington, Mass.: Bellman, 1977); *Study Abroad*. 21st ed. (New York: UNESCO, 1977); Nancy Young and Mary Louise Taylor, eds. *Study in Europe: Handbook on International Study for U.S. Nationals* (New York: Institute of International Education, 1976).

3. Paul Wasserman, ed. *Awards, Honors and Prizes: A Directory and Source Book* (Detroit: Gale Research, 1969). For language and literature, see the article by S. F. Johnson, "Honors and Prizes in the MLA Field," *PMLA* 67 (February 1952): 37-58.

Grants in the Humanities

Scholar's Guide to Funding Sources

1 The Art of Grantsmanship

GENERAL

The first thing that the humanist interested in earning grant support for research must keep in mind is that the approach to the process of securing a grant is like that to any other business venture. That is, there must be the willingness to spend the time necessary for self-education—in this case, in the art of grantsmanship. That art involves the ability to prepare an effective grant proposal. Not only must the proposal be carefully researched and accompanied by a well-prepared budget, but the research description must be written in such a way as to show that the applicant knows the field and has chosen a research topic that is reasonable as well as capable of adding significantly to the store of human knowledge or of improving the human condition. The second thing that the humanist should keep in mind—and this is by way of encouragement—is that earning grant support is much like picking olives from a jar: the first is always most difficult, while the rest come easier. Like all other human entities, foundations need to be reassured about their choices. Nothing reassures more than the judgment of others, coupled, of course, with the continued good work of the grant applicant.

FINDING THE SOURCES OF SUPPORT

The identification of the sources most likely to fund research projects in one's area of study is the first step. Those teaching in universities which have grant funds of their own should first seek this support. For those teaching at universities that employ a director of research, the suggestions and guidance through the process of applying for grant funds from this officer can be invaluable. The advice of colleagues is also beneficial. But whatever the guidance that can be derived from others, it is to the advantage of the humanist to obtain as much first-hand knowledge about the process of applying for grant funds as possible.

The many guides to grant-funding sources are a valuable source of information (an annotated bibliography of the most important of these sources is included at the end of this chapter), but the problem here is one of volume: the variety of such printed information is enormous. And, although specialized grants lists are published in certain areas of the humanities, like literature, history, and philosophy,[1] no general guide exists for all of the humanities. This guide hopes to fill that gap.

IDENTIFYING SUITABLE GRANT SOURCES

The foundations listed in Appendix A of this guide are those whose major commitment is to support research, scholarship, or artistic endeavor in one or more of the humanities. In attempting to isolate a suitable foundation from this list, one should rely on the index, which has been carefully cross-referenced from particular humanities areas to the names of the agencies funding in those areas.

There are, of course, thousands of other foundations in the United States and Canada. Some limit themselves to a specific geographical area, while others concern themselves only peripherally with the humanities. The labor involved in identifying all these foundations would not have been worth the result, since most of the foundations involved would be of no use to the vast majority of the readers of this guide. But the means for identifying these foundations are provided. Essentially, one can discover the names of small and local grants-making agencies by using the resources of the Foundation Center. The publications of the Center and the addresses of its national and regional collections are described in Appendix D.

Whatever combination of these sources of information a researcher uses, a careful reading of the foundation's self-description is essential. Many a grant seeker has wasted time because of failure to discover that a foundation is interested only in those with a superior publishing record, a completed doctorate, membership in a specific learned society, or residence in a specific geographical area. Many foundations change their areas of interest or their application procedures, so that the time invested in finding out as much background about a foundation is time well invested.

When one's list has been narrowed down to the approximate and most suitable sources, the next step is to acquire the most up to the minute information about the grant program for which one is applying. Many foundations publish descriptive brochures which are available on request. These often list the most recent projects supported—providing another indication of the most current interests of a funding agency. (This information is also available in foundations' annual reports, which are available at the libraries of the Foundation Center.)

PRELIMINARY CONTACTS

Often some preliminary contact with a granting agency is in order at this point. One could call or, even better, write the agency, describing the project briefly and asking whether the agency would be interested in considering a fully developed proposal. (This process is, by the way, necessary in grant applications to the National Endowment for the Arts and the National Endowment for the Humanities. NEA and NEH require a preliminary screening of applicants, through the exchange of brief project descriptions, before they forward formal application papers.) The advantage of such a process is that it can save the applicant's time if the agency is not interested in that particular research area. The process can also provide valuable information about how to organize a proposal in such a way as to suit the requirements of the agency. I have found that this process has been particularly helpful in dealing with NEH and NEA. Each time I forwarded preliminary grant applications to these agencies, I received detailed critiques of these outlines, suggestions on how to arrange them in terms of Endowment requirements, and even an appraisal of the chances of success of the project in relation to similar ones which were currently seeking support. A final advantage of a preliminary contact with an agency is that it often provides a name —a person whom one can consult as problems arise in the preparation of a proposal. In one instance, when I was unable to complete a proposal in time to meet a deadline, my contact in the granting agency arranged for an extension. So, for a variety of important reasons, the applicant should certainly become known to the funding agency at an early date.

NOTES:

[1] "Fellowship and Grants," is published annually in the September issue of *PMLA* (Publications of the Modern Language Association); the American Historical Association publishes an annual booklet, *Grants and Fellowships of Interest to Historians,* at a cost of $3; $4 to nonmembers. The American Philosophical Association distributes an annual brochure, *Fellowships and Grant Opportunities of Interest to Philosophers,* for free.

A DESCRIPTIVE BIBLIOGRAPHY OF RESEARCH GRANTS AND FELLOWSHIPS

For further information about a specific grant source, consult the *Annual Register, The Grants Register, The Foundation Directory, Foundation Grants to Individuals, Directory of Research Grants,* and (for Federal programs) *Catalog of Federal Domestic Assistance,* which are described below. Excluded from this list are publications which do not deal primarily with the humanities and which describe grants programs for institutions and organizations.

General:

Annual Register of Grant Support. Chicago: Marquis Academic Media, 1969—. Annual. $57.50. With *The Grants Register,* this is the best *general* guide for the researcher. The *Annual Register* contains information on major foundations in the arts, sciences, and humanities along with full financial and statistical information on each foundation listed.

Catalog of Federal Domestic Assistance. Washington, D.C.: Government Printing Office. Annual. $20. A compendium of over 1000 Federal programs, projects, services, and activities that provide assistance or benefits to the American public. Over 450 of these programs accept grant proposals from individuals. Each listing provides general information on the program and information about other government resources in the same subject area.

Directory of Research Grants. William K. Wilson and Betty L. Wilson, eds. Phoenix: Oryx. Annual. $37.50. A list of about 2000 programs that provide grants, contracts, and fellowships for research, training, and program development. Out of the 85 areas indexed, 15 are humanities-related. Although similar in scope to the *Annual Register,* it emphasizes college and university grants.

The Foundation Directory. 7th ed. Marianna O. Lewis, ed. New York: Columbia University Pr. for the Foundation Center, 1979. $40. Arranged by states, this lists the name, address, purpose, and financial data (assets, expenditures, total number of grants in most recent years) of all American foundations. Provides a general index of fields of interest.

The Foundation Grants Index Annual: A Cumulative Listing of Foundation Grants. Lee Noe, ed. New York: Columbia University Pr. for the Foundation Center, 1972—. Annual. $20. Lists statistics on 15,000 grants awarded almost entirely to institutions by 390 major foundations in a single year, and includes brief grant descriptions and subject index. Although many researchers are often directed to this book, it is not valuable for the individual.

Foundation Grants to Individuals. 2nd ed. New York: Foundation Center, 1979. $15. Like other publications of the Foundation Center, this emphasizes statistics instead of program descriptions and application information. To be used together with *Grants in the Humanities.*

The Grants Register: 1979–1981. Roland Turner, ed. New York: St. Martin's Pr., 1978. $26.50. A first-rate guide for the researcher, this is more international in scope than the *Annual Register,* and contains superb indexes.

The National Directory of Grants and Aid to Individuals in the Arts, International. 3rd ed. Daniel Millsaps et al. eds. Washington, D.C.: Washington International Arts Letter, 1976. $13.95. Not generally suited to humanists, this is a finding list of grants, prizes, awards, and scholarships for professional work in the arts. It contains no commentary or information on programs.

Foreign Foundations:

Fellowship Guide to Western Europe. 4th ed. New York: Council for European Studies, 1978. $3. This guide is good for students, faculty, and researchers in the social sciences and humanities who wish to study or do research in western Europe either in residence at a specific university or as an independent researcher.
The Grants Register. See above.
Guide to European Foundations. Milano: Fondazione Giovanni Agnelli (New York: Columbia University Pr.), 1973. $20. A revised edition of *Directory of European Foundations* (1969). Includes a bibliography and indexes.
The International Foundation Directory. H. V. Hodson, ed. 2nd ed. Gale: Detroit, 1979. Provides general descriptions of activities of large foundations throughout the world, including statistical information. Contains a bibliography and indexes.

Women's Studies and Projects:

Where to Find Foundation Money for Women's Projects: A Directory to Who's Giving Money to Women's Projects. Edith L. Adams, comp. Yonkers, N.Y.: Independent Women's Pr., 1977. A finding list under broad topics, this publication contains no statistics or commentary.

A DESCRIPTIVE BIBLIOGRAPHY OF GRANTSMANSHIP

For further *general* information about the art of winning foundation grants, consult the following works:

General:

Grantsmanship: Money and How to Get It. 2nd ed. Chicago: Marquis Academic Media, 1978. $7.50. More suited for the professional grantsman than for the amateur, this describes services of various agencies which aid the professional grantsman. It also contains an excellent bibliography.
Howard Hillman and Karin Abarbanel. *The Art of Winning Foundation Grants.* New York: Vanguard, 1975. $7.95. A practical, general guide.
Virginia P. White. *Grants: How to Find Out About Them and What to Do Next.* New York: Plenum, 1975. $19.50. Reviews current activities of foundations and federal government grant programs, describes history and development of grant programs, and includes a three-part section on the grant-making process.

For the Professional Grantsman:

Foundation Reporter: A Method for Keeping Current on Foundations. Jean Brodsky, ed. Washington, D.C.: Taft. Annual. $275. Includes National Edition and several regional volumes. This is a superbly organized list of grants to institutions and organizations—not to individuals.

Grantsmanship Center News. A slickly edited magazine on all phases of professional grantsmanship. With a circulation of above 40,000, this is the most widely read periodical in the field. (The Grantsmanship Center, 1031 South Grand Ave., Los Angeles, Calif. 90015, which publishes the *Center News,* also conducts training programs nationwide in the various aspects of grantsmanship.)

Grantsmanship: Money and How to Get It. See above.

2 Writing the Proposal

GENERAL

Writing the proposal is the most critical step in the process of obtaining grant support. The proposal is the only means a granting agency has of evaluating the worth of a project. No matter what the applicant's intelligence, enthusiasm, or ability to bring a project to completion, unless these can be expressed in a convincing way, the project has no chance of being funded.

The applicant must remember that the proposal should be intelligible both to generalists and to specialists. In some foundations, proposals are read first by those who are generally familiar with a field, but who are by no means experts in it. Only if the proposal passes through a first review is it sent to specialists in its area of study. Other foundations reverse the process, sending it first to the specialists and then to the generalists for a final review. So the proposal should be written as a self-contained object. That is, its reviewers should be able to understand it without recourse to other persons or other data. This will demand a writing style that is logical but not pedantic, clear but not condescending.

SCOPE

The first thing all researchers must keep firmly in mind before proceeding to develop a prospectus is the *scope* of the project. That is, they must be able to identify specifically the object which they hope to achieve. If a project is only a preliminary study, it should be identified as such. If the discoveries might open up areas of investigation which the research project is not equipped to handle, this should be clarified somewhere in the proposal. If the project is designed to clarify a problem instead of creating a solution, this also should be made clear.

Many projects have not been funded because they promised results totally impractical, given the personnel and resources of the proposal. Others who have been granted funds have found themselves in the unenviable position of not being able to produce the grandiose results they promised in their grant prospectuses. As a result, they either abandoned the project or produced results less than they had promised, in both instances harming their reputations.

It is best to be quite realistic about what one can achieve in a given grant period. This indicates to the reviewers of the project that the applicant has thought it through with care. It also improves one's chances for subsequent funding from the same or from a different foundation, since the researcher can demonstrate that the work promised under one foundation grant was, in fact, produced.

ORGANIZATION

The grant proposal should include the following, paginated in sequence:

1. title page or face sheet (including abstract)
2. table of contents
3. research design (description of proposed project)
4. time schedule
5. budget
6. addenda

The purpose of this is to answer the following questions:

What do you want to do?
Why do you want to do it?
How are you going to do it?
Who is going to do it?
Where are you going to do it?
How long will it take?
How much will it cost?
What significant contribution will it make to the field?

THE PROPOSAL

I. Title Page

It is important that the applicant learn the granting agency's format for a grant proposal. Many agencies, and the federal government inevitably, have standardized title page forms for including all the necessary information of the proposal. An *abstract* is usually a feature of the title page. This is a helpful device, particularly if the application is long. The abstract is a clear and concise statement of what problem the project will address and what it attempts to accomplish. The abstract should outline the main features of the project, using a minimum of professional jargon. Finally, it should contain an objective assessment of the importance of the project. If the title page does not call for an abstract, it would be wise to include one at the beginning of the research design. All this is to be paginated in sequence, as an aid in your own cross-references within the proposal and also to aid the reviewers of the proposal.

II. Research Design

The research design is a full-scale version of the abstract. It is the heart of the proposal. In form, it should resemble the newspaper story, with the most important information first, instead of the scholarly article, which reserves the conclusions to the end. Presuming that the abstract to the proposal narrative has captured a reviewer's attention, the applicant must then strive, like some wise and patient guide, to lead the reviewer through the complexities of the proposal that follows. The applicant's most important function throughout this is to anticipate any intelligent objections that a reviewer might make about the project. One convenient way of organizing the research design is in two steps: the statement of a problem and the statement of a solution.

The Beginning Problem

In the body of the proposal, the applicant should point out a gap or a problem in a particular field of knowledge or of human endeavor—the one with which this project will deal. This part of the application should include information about related work in the field and work in progress. The point of this is to reassure the reviewer that one is familiar with the work in the area. If the applicant can briefly quote any of the authorities in a field about this particular problem, their comments should be included.

The Method of Solving the Problem

Having established that a problem exists, the applicant must then set out to show how, given funding, he or she will go about solving that problem: by publishing research, organizing a course of study, arranging a performance, and so on. The method of investigating the problem will be the invention of the investigator. The applicant's aim in describing this is to outline a method of investigation that is logical, that is realistic, and that foresees all intelligent objections. If the reviewer is with the applicant to this point, the proposal will stand or fall at this description of method. For it is here that the applicant is revealed as knowledgeable in the field and confident in using its tools and method of research. And it is also at this point that the applicant is revealed as capable of producing the results of the research which the agency is being asked to fund.

So, in organizing the description of method, the applicant should certainly seek the help of colleagues or of experts in a given field. I would add at this point that my experience in seeking the help of well-known scholars in a variety of research areas has always been positive. I have found that scholars of international reputation are generally quite willing to offer advice on specific problems and to encourage younger scholars in their field of research. Some have even written letters of recommendation, based on a project description. Naturally, it is taken for granted that the researcher already has the research design in mind and has done all the preliminary work before consulting an expert about technical problems in a research project or about a letter of recommendation.

III. Time Schedule

The next logical step in the construction of a grant proposal is a detailed listing of the practical means of completing the project. This spells out the precise means by which the "solution" to the problem will be carried out. The first piece of technical information, then, should be a *time schedule*. This is a statement indicating the total length of time the project will take. The statement should be broken down to indicate the timing of the separate phases of the project.

IV. Budget

The budget is the second essential part of the proposal. If the research design has convinced the reviewer that a project deserves consideration, the budget design will convince the reviewer whether it ought to be funded. The research design and the budget are linked in tandem, for the budget spells out in concrete terms the means by which the research is to be realized. The budget, therefore, refers constantly to the information supplied in the research design.

A note, before proceeding to a description of the budget. It is helpful to include in a budget justification for any expense that is not immediately self-explanatory. (Even salaries must be explained, with a notation whether the investigator will be receiving sabbatical pay and how the salary figure was arrived at. Certainly something like a large long-distance telephone expenditure might need some explanation.) Any item that needs further explanation or justification should be indicated in the budget by an asterisk. The justification of these items should appear in an addendum to the budget. This should be very specific. The applicant must explain *why* the expense is necessary. One other function of such a budget justification would be to indicate that the applicant has researched the subject seriously.

A. Direct Costs

1. Personnel and Salaries.

The first necessary information concerns personnel and salaries. Personnel whose services involve some kind of compensation under the grant should be listed by name, position, and title (within the project). This will be followed by a description of their experience (if this has not been indicated by their position), the responsibilities within the project, the percentage of their time to be committed to the activity, and their salaries. (Salaries are based on the percentage of one's normal academic salary that is devoted to research under the grant. A corresponding release from other duties is not mandatory.) The salary should be accompanied by a breakdown of the corresponding fringe benefits (see 2. below).

Key staff members should be listed by name and their resumes attached as *addenda* (see Section V.). If this is not possible, brief job descriptions with a listing of the competencies necessary should be provided in that attachment. Principal investigators should be listed, followed by other professional project staff, nonprofessional project staff, student research assistants, and consultants.

2. Fringe benefits.

These include social security, unemployment insurance, medical coverage, and pension benefits for employees.

In humanities grants proposals, which often involve one or two principal investigators who are already employed full-time at a university, the business of fringe benefits is often less of a problem than in more complex grants. Aside from the mandatory social security contribution for salaries, grant applicants do not often have to concern themselves about fringe benefits for employees who work less than 20 hours a week. But in any case, one must check institutional guidelines in this matter. Consultants and others who receive "stipends" or "fees" have no fringe benefits. Students often do, depending on institutional policy.

If a grant applicant is a faculty member at a university that has established an office of grants and contracts to oversee the administration of grants, then the office's guidelines should be followed. The point to keep in mind, though, is that the question of fringe benefits with the funding agency and with one's academic institution (which will be administering the grant) should be explored before completing the proposed budget.

3. Computer time.

If a research project involves the use of computers, the costs involved should be calculated accurately. The cost of coders, programmers, and the like should be included in the salary budget with fringe benefits, if appropriate. The computer costs can thus be used as part of the base for overhead costs (see B, below). Computer time should not be used for cost sharing (see H, below) unless this is required by the funding agency.

4. Equipment.

Equipment estimates should be as precise as possible. In an era of changing prices, one should also remember that a delivery date may be as much as a year after the proposal is written. Remember, too, that many universities have their own buying services which often provide substantial discounts. When a grant operates on campus, the special facilities involved or the installation of new equipment will require college approval. Agreements covering this must be worked out before a grant is submitted. Finally, the ownership of equipment used in a research project may vary. The funding agency may claim it, the title may pass to the university, or in some cases, it becomes the property of the project director.

5. Supplies and communications.

This category includes all "consumable" items: long-distance telephone, telegrams, postage, duplication, stationery, reference works, special services provided by one's university, and the like. The items may be arranged appropriate to the particular grant. The point to remember is that the need for these—as for all budget costs—must be apparent somewhere in the proposal.

6. Travel.

Examiners tend to scrutinize travel budgets carefully, so the applicant should be certain that the proposal leaves no doubt that travel is essential to the completion of the project. Funds cover travel over only the most direct route.

a. Transportation Charges. In working out transportation charges, one should keep the following restrictions in mind:

airline:	limited to economy fare
railroad:	lower-berth for overnight travel; parlor car for day travel

car rental: basic rental plus mileage charge plus
               tolls; round trip cost must not exceed
               round trip economy air or train costs
local travel: taxis, bus fare, and the like will be
               reimbursed as required .

b. *Domestic Subsistence.* Domestic subsistence expenses are for food, lodging, and related costs. U.S. State Department guidelines for domestic and foreign subsistence are a good example to follow if guidance is needed. At present, the federal government uses a sliding scale, depending on the city. These figures should be available at the grants office. The figure might increase, so the applicant should check with the institutional officer when submitting an application.

c. *Foreign Subsistence.* State Department guidelines for subsistence costs incurred during foreign travel are also on a sliding scale that varies from country to country and often from city to city within the same country. (For example, during 1979 daily subsistence in Rome was $68 per day, but was $72 per day in Florence.) These guidelines are revised every several months. A campus research director should have the current figures, which are also available at the various Foundation Center offices. The document listing these rates is called: "Standardized Regulations/Government-Civilians/Foreign Areas" and is available through the Department of State, Washington, D.C. 20520; 202-235-9519, 9516. Other expenses related to business travel and necessary to the purpose of the trip such as phone calls, baggage charges, red-cap services, registration fees for professional meetings, and stenographic services in connection with preparing travel reports are reimbursable.

7. *Publication and report costs.*

Costs of preparing and distributing a *final report* should be included. In smaller grants this is most often a negligible expense, but larger grants require more elaborate reports. Page costs and related items necessary for publication of the research in learned journals may be included. Some granting agencies maintain a separate fund for this purpose, to which a grantee may apply when the research is accepted for publication. So, if publication costs are allowable, an applicant should inquire how the agency deals with them.

B. Indirect Costs

Indirect costs are the same as overhead. They are the administrative costs—to the university—of running a program. When a university is involved in a grant proposal, it obligates itself to certain costs connected with the grant. These could be the use and maintenance of office space where grant research is conducted, plus purchasing, accounting, and payroll services for the grant. These indirect costs must be in every grant proposal. These are three types of indirect funding.

1. One employs the federal government formula based on a percentage of salaries and wages in the grant.

2. Some funding agencies mandate other alternatives, based on a different percentage or taking a percentage of a different base figure in the budget. Many colleges and universities now use a "modified total direct cost" system.

3. Other agencies negotiate a fixed-fee contract with the university or with the university foundation overseeing the grant.

This information might seem confusing to the scholar trying to become familiar with the process of organizing a grant proposal. But one should be aware that indirect costs are a necessary part of the grant budget. In preparing this section of the budget, it would be best to seek out the services of a grant coordinator or of some university fiscal officer who is sophisticated in grants administration.

C. Cost-Sharing

While paying the university the costs of administering and overseeing a grant, many foundations require something in return from the university. This is a contribution to the grant of some goods or services that would normally be included in the budget and is know as *cost-sharing*. Since many universities feel that it is better to receive than to give, they tend to be unhappy about cost-sharing. So, naturally, it is a subject for the grant applicant to avoid if possible.

Like the matter of indirect costs, cost-sharing, when required, demands the involvement of university personnel. And like indirect costs, the cost-sharing rate is negotiable. The university's part of cost-sharing can be managed in several ways. Often it involves the contribution to the grant of the full or part-time services of a secretary or other personnel. Sometimes, too, the amount can be covered by the purchase for the university library of a selection of books relating to the grant subject. If the indirect cost rate for the grant is less than the suggested federal rate, the difference between the federal rate and the agreed rate can often be "donated" by the university to the grant as its part of the cost-sharing.

A final note about budget costs: in a misguided effort to improve one's chance to receive funding, the applicant should not underestimate the costs. In practice, foundations often trim some of the budget of a proposal. Such reductions of an already unrealistic budget might put such an applicant in the position of being unable to complete the work. In working up a budget, the applicant should estimate the costs realistically, planning for increased costs and fluctuations in currency (for proposals involving foreign research). The grant seeker must not hesitate to include whatever costs that are justified.

V. Addenda

Addenda to the grant proposal should be all those documents which support the grant, but which, because of their length, would interfere with the "argument" of the grant. A few examples would be:

   a. a *curriculum vitae* of the principal investigators
   b. letters of recommendation supporting the project
   c. letters of commitment from universities, publishers, and organizations connected with the project
   d. correspondence in regard to the project

VI. Signatures

Many grants require institutional approvals in the form of a co-signature or certification of the project by the president or a designee. Occasionally, one hears of the grant applicant who, in the flurry of last-minute assembly of the grant proposal, neglected to get the necessary co-signature and had the grant application returned after its deadline. In these days, when college presidents are often away from their institutions, the situation might arise that a president is not available when a signature is required. It is the grant applicant's responsibility, therefore, to make certain that the institutional representative or a deputy is available when a signature is required.

Sending the Proposal to the Agency

Every effort should be made to insure that the proposal, with all supporting documents, reaches the funding agency before its deadline. If some extraordinary problem intervenes, though, it is better to seek an extension from the agency than to throw a proposal together and thus damage its chances. In these circumstances, one can request an extension through one's contact in the granting agency, as discussed in Chapter One.

It is often wise to include a covering letter in the proposal package. This is particularly true if the agency has suggested any changes in the research design or the budget or if any negotiations have been involved in the preparation of the proposal. The letter should refer to the agency personnel involved and to the modifications that have been made. (This will guarantee that those who have been involved with the project in its earlier stages will continue to be involved with it.)

Before submitting the proposal, the applicant—or, better still, someone who has not been so closely connected with every stage of the proposal—should read it carefully, checking for typographical errors and checking the budget figures. A final review should insure that the proposal contains all its parts in proper order and that the package includes the number of copies of the proposal which the foundation requires. If any other supporting material does not accompany the proposal, the applicant should see that this reaches the foundation in time. (Do not hesitate to call a foundation to ask whether all materials for a proposal have been received.) The whole package should be sent by registered mail, with a return receipt requested. Remember, though, that this will take an extra day or two in the mails.

3 The Sample Proposal

Following is a complete humanities proposal, including all supporting material. The specific subject of the grant proposal, 14th and 15th century Italian humanism, is of professional interest to only a few readers of this book. But an actual proposal such as this can help to crystallize in the reader's mind much of the theoretical information contained in the previous chapter. The proposal is commented on and explained on the facing pages. The proposal is followed by a more general example of a proposal budget. This, too, can act as a concrete and specific example of a budget for the reader who might be somewhat bewildered by all the technical information in Chapter Two. A bibliography of proposal writing concludes the chapter.

APPLICATION FOR A PSC-BHE RESEARCH AWARD

		Review Panel*		Number	
This application is for:		Italian			
Annual Award:	☒ New	Name (First)	(Initial)	(Last)	
		John	W.	SMITH	
	☐ Renewal	Department		College	
		English		John Jay	
	☐ Contingency	Rank		Telephone No.	
Award Period:	Human Subjects:	Associate		Office: 910-1112	
July 1979 – June 1980	☐ Yes ☒ No	Professor		Home: 234-5678	
	Animals:	Home Address (include ZIP code)			
	☐ Yes ☒ No	2345 Sixth Street			
Amount Requested $1543.68		New York, New York 10003			

Title of proposed project

A Descriptive Catalogue of the Manuscript Commentaries on Boccaccio's <u>Teseida</u>

Brief Abstract of proposed project. Confine description to this space. The grant will underwrite a descriptive catalogue of the 18 Italian manuscripts with commentaries of Giovanni Boccaccio's <u>Teseida</u>: Boccaccio's own commentary (c. 1350; 12 MSS), that of Pietro Andrea de' Bassi (c. 1425; 4 MSS), and two anonymous 15th century commentaries (1 MS each). Boccaccio's <u>Teseida</u> was the first imitation of the classical epic form in a modern European tongue. The commentaries on the <u>Teseida</u> were needed to explain to early humanists the allusions to classical--and particularly Greek--myth. The study will be a valuable contribution to the history of humanism. It will establish the relationships and textual history of the manuscripts with commentaries by Boccaccio and de' Bassi. It will make available descriptions of two anonymous commentaries which have never before been edited or described. It will provide for scholars a body of previously unknown information about the extent of the knowledge of classical myth and literature in the West during the first century of humanistic study.

APPLICANT'S CERTIFICATION:
It is understood and agreed by the applicant:
1. That the award may be revoked in whole or in part should the recipient's relationship with the City University cease to exist provided that such revocation shall not include any amounts obligated previous to the effective date of revocation.
2. That the general terms and conditions of this proposal as stated in the application form, program guidelines and elsewhere have been read and accepted.
3. That any funds granted as a result of this application are to be expended for the purpose outlined herein in accordance with University and Foundation policies, and any funds not expended for this purpose shall revert to the PSC-BHE Research Award Program upon completion or termination of award, whichever is earlier.

Applicant's Signature _John W. Smith_   Date _31 October 1978_

CAMPUS ENDORSEMENT:
This is to certify that the applicant is authorized to conduct the study described by the accompanying proposal on this campus, and that the undersigned is satisfied that the scope of the applicant's project will not interfere with his professional duties. The following facilities or other support will be provided on campus to assist this study:

Signature _John G. Michlund_ Title _Director - office of Sponsor Program_ Date _10/31/78_

RF 400 7/79 Rev.   *See list in Guidelines

Abstract provides a brief introduction to the project, some general or background information about the text under discussion, and a statement of the value and importance of the work to be done.

Required *institutional signature.*

PSC-BHE Research Award Program

Table of Contents

N.B. Page Numbers For Sections After Budget
To Be Filled In By The Applicant

Table of Contents simplifies the work of the grant and of those who must review the project.

PSC-BHE RESEARCH AWARD PROGRAM

Name: John William SMITH

Rank:

Academic Year Salary: $ 22,030.00

College: John Jay

Proposed Grant Period

From: July 1979

Through: June 1980

Department: English

Title of Proposed Project:

A Descriptive Catalogue of the Manuscript Commentaries on Boccaccio's <u>Teseida</u>

Proposed Budget

Salaries and Wages
Principal Investigator (Summer Salary) _____ _____
Other professional (indicate title) _____
_____
_____ _____

Secretary _____ _____
Other non-professional (indicate title)   <u>typist</u>
160 hrs. @ $4.01   646.40

Sub-Total		
Fringe Benefits (20%)	129.28	
	TOTAL SALARIES AND FRINGES	$775.68

Equipment — Nonexpendable _____ _____

Supplies — Expendable _____ paper _____   40.00

Duplication, Xeroxing _____ _____

Travel
Transportation (Mode-Destination(s)) _____

Estimated Per Diem Expenses* _____ _____
Other _____
TOTAL TRAVEL   300.00

Other (list) ___ conversion of 15 pos. to neg. microfilms @ $20.00 ___
____ printing of 18 negative microfilms @ $18.00   324.00
____ binding of 18 printed microfilms @ $3.00   54.00

____ postage   50.00
TOTAL BUDGET $1543.68

*Provide itinerary (approximate dates and duration at each location) in budget justification.

*(Please check with Guidelines for explanations of budget items
listed above. A detailed budget justification should follow.)*

RF 401 7/79 Rev.

Time Schedule: many agencies require a more elaborate step-by-step explanation of how the grant time is to be used. In cases where the kind of time schedule is not specified, it is best to provide a more detailed one.

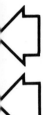

Under this program's guidelines, not all applicants are eligible for *summer salary.*

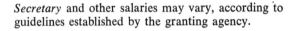

Secretary and other salaries may vary, according to guidelines established by the granting agency.

Fringe benefits are social security, health insurance, pension, unemployment insurance, etc. Sometimes these must be listed separately; more often, though, the granting agency or the institutional research foundation which administers the grant sets a fixed percentage of salaries for fringe benefits. Sometimes this rate varies, depending on job title, whether the position is full or part time, etc.

Budget Justification

Typist

In order to collate the 12 MSS with Boccaccio's commentary and the 4 MSS with de' Bassi's commentary, a typist must reproduce these two long commentaries on large collation sheets. This person will also type my transcription of the two unique and anonymous commentaries which have not yet been published. The greatest part of this will be the typing of the 123 folio commentary in the Paris MS. This commentary alone will produce several hundred pages of typescript.

The typist should be bi-lingual.

Estimated is four weeks' typing @ 40 hours/week.

Should the typist's work be completed before four weeks, that person will be used as a reader to aid in collating the manuscripts. A reader was employed in the extensive collating necessary for the Chaucer Library Teseida. This was found to be an efficient process and a means of avoiding errors.

Paper

Included in this item were the large collation sheets and the typing paper necessary to reproduce the two anonymous commentaries.

Microfilms

The estimates were supplied by the Independent Printing Service, 215 E. 42nd Street, New York.
Conversion of 15 positive microfilms to negatives:
In order to be printed a microfilm must be a negative. Of the 18 microfilms which I already have, 15 are positive copies.
15 microfilms x $20 (conversion charge per microfilm) = $300.00

Printing of 18 negative microfilms:
Cost: 18¢ per linear foot of printed text
Each microfilm was estimated to produce 100 feet of printed text.
100 ft. x 18¢ per ft. x 18 microfilms = $324.00

Binding of xerox printouts of microfilms is necessary to prevent loss of pages and damage to paper: 18 @ $3.00/printout = $54.00
Price was based on large format of pages.

Postage

This item was necessary for correspondence with manuscript curators to ascertain information about binding, watermarks, folio gatherings, and other physical information that a microfilm cannot provide. The information is necessary for the catalogue descriptions. $50.00

Other Funding

An application for support of the project has been made to the Summer Stipend program, Division of Fellowships, National Endowment for the Humanities.

that budget justification assumes no prior knowledge on the part of the
~wer. The attempt here is not only to explain *what* each item means, but,
important, *why* it is essential to the project.

The description of the *typist's* job justifies the need of a
secretary; this item constitutes more than half of the
budget and therefore would merit the reviewer's scrutiny.
Since the project depends on the secretary's work, the need
for a typist must be explained at some length.

This anticipates the question, how the secretary's time will
be used *if the typing is completed* within less than the
budgeted four weeks.

This explanation of *microfilm* costs indicates that this item
is not a mere estimate; demonstrates the seriousness,
thoroughness, and experience of the applicant.

Postage is described to assure the budget reviewer that
this is a necessary item.

Information on *other funding* is required by the
granting agency.

Prior PSC-BHE Awards

                         publications generated

Summer 1971   # 1400   Philippe de Mézières' Campaign for the Feast of

                       Mary's Presentation. Toronto Medieval Latin

                       Texts. University of Toronto, in press

Summer 1972   # 1559   The Play of Mary: A 14th Century Music Drama

                       (performing edition)

                       performances at:

                         Graduate School of Music

                         Indiana University

                         Bloomington, Indiana   12 August 1976

                         Curitiba Festival, Brazil   January 1977

Summer 1973   # 10021 Giovanni Boccaccio. Il Teseida. Chaucer Library

Summer 1974   # 10553 Edition. University of Georgia Press. forth-

                       coming.

                       "Chaucer, the Teseida, and the Visconti Library

                       at Pavia." Medium Aevum. forthcoming 1979.

As indicated previously, an application for support of this project
from the National Endowment for the Humanities is pending.

This information is required by the granting agency. Note that the *past grants* are not merely listed. The attempt here is to demonstrate that prior grants from the same agency have produced practical results as, presumably, would the present grant request, if funded.

Curriculum Vitae

John William SMITH
2345 Sixth Street
New York, New York 10003

(212) 234-5678

1. Education
    1970. Ph.D. English Literature. City University of New York
           Dissertation: "On the Discrimination of Gothicisms"

    1966. M.A. English Literature. University of Virginia
           Thesis: "The Knight's Tale: A Search for the Ordered Universe"

    1965. A.B. English Literature. Providence College

    1962. A.A. Latin and Greek. St. Joseph Seminary

2. Academic Honors
    Visiting Scholar. Institute for Advanced Study, Princeton.
        Summers 1971, 1978

    Grants:
        National Endowment for the Humanities. Summer 1970.
          (project completed; see section 4)

        American Council of Learned Societies. Summer 1972.
          (project completed; see section 4)

        Research Foundation. City University of New York. Summers 1971-74.
          (projects completed; see sections 4a1, 4a2, 4e)

    DuPont Fellow. University of Virginia. 1965-1966.

3. Employment
    1976-present.   Associate Professor of English
    1970-1975.   Assistant Professor of English,
                 John Jay College of Criminal Justice
                 City University of New York

    1969-1970.   Instructor of English
                 Suffolk County Community College

    1967-1969.   Lecturer (part-time) in English
                 Queensborough Community College

    1966-1968.   Lecturer (part-time) in English
                 Hunter College

Education indicates preparation to do proposed project.

Past grants are explained on the next page, to indicate that they have had practical results.

Employment record starts with most recent position.

4. Published Work and Completed Research
   a. books   1. Philippe de Mézières' Campaign for the Feast of Mary's
                  Presentation. Toronto Medieval Latin texts. Univer-
                  sity of Toronto. in press. (edition and commentary
                  of Paris, Bib. Nat. MSS lat. 17330 and 14454; research
                  sponsored by NEH grant, Summer 1970, and by CUNY
                  Research Foundation grant, Summer 1971)
               2. Giovanni Boccaccio. Il Teseida. Chaucer Library
                  Edition. co-editor. forthcoming. University of
                  Georgia. (research sponsored by CUNY Research Founda-
                  tion grants, Summers 1973, 1974)

   b. articles 1. "Chaucer, the Teseida, and the Visconti Library at
                  Pavia" Medium Aevum. forthcoming 1979.
               2. "Drama, Middle English" and "Digby Plays" in Artemis
                  Lexikon des Mittelalters. in fasc. 1976-.

   c. introduction to M. Harley. Priory of St. Bernard. Gothic Reprints
      Series. Arno Press. 1977. p. xviij.

   d. reviews of "The Book of Kells" (Pictura Films) and "English Hand-
      writing in the Dark Ages" (University of Toronto).
      Ralph: For Teaching Medieval and Renaissance Humanities.
      3 (October 1976): 4, 6.

   e. Performances:
                  The Play of Mary: A 14th Century Music Drama
                     (playscript of performing edition)

                     Graduate School of Music
                     Indiana University, Bloomington, Indiana
                     12 August 1976

                     Curitiba Festival, Brazil
                     January 1977

                     (research for performing edition sponsored by ACLS
                     grant and by CUNY Research Foundation grant, Summer
                     1972)

   f. lectures pertinent to proposed research topic:
                  11/4/78 "Giovanni Boccaccio: Scribe and Transmittor of
                           Humanist Texts"
                           World of Boccaccio Colloquium. Mercy College

                  11/5/77 "Boccaccio Manuscripts in the Visconti Library
                           at Pavia"
                           World of Boccaccio Colloquium. Mercy College

                  10/7/77 "The Search for Chaucer's Teseida"
                           Medieval Club of New York

                  4/20/75 "Boccaccio in Medieval England"
                           International Boccaccio Symposium.
                           Fordham University

                  12/26/74 "The Chaucer Library Edition of Boccaccio's
                           Teseida"
                           American Boccaccio Association

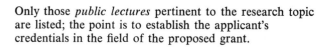

Publishing record indicates applicant's experience in proposed field of research; it also demonstrates that *prior grants* have produced positive scholarly results as, presumably, would the proposed grant.

Only those *public lectures* pertinent to the research topic are listed; the point is to establish the applicant's credentials in the field of the proposed grant.

Project Description

Background

Giovanni Boccaccio's _Teseida_ (c. 1341) was the first imitation of
the classical epic in a modern European language. Boccaccio apparently
circulated the first manuscript(s) of the _Teseida_ without any commentary.
But in the early 1350s, at the same time he was working on the _Genealogia
deorum gentilium_, Boccaccio produced a manuscript of the _Teseida_ with
his own commentary on the work. This manuscript was identified only
fifty years ago, when the Italian government purchased it from a private
collection.[1] The holograph of the _Teseida_ was deposited in the Laurentian
Library in Florence, where it is presently Cod. Acquisti e Doni 325.

The discovery of a copy of the work in Boccaccio's hand and with
Boccaccio's commentary inspired new scholarship on the _Teseida_.[2] The
manuscript, including the commentary, has been edited three times in
the past forty years: by Salvatore Battaglia (Accademia della Crusca:
Florence 1938), by Aurelio Roncaglia (Bari 1941), and by Alberto Limen-
tani (Milan 1964).

My previous work with the _Teseida_ has been as co-editor of the
forthcoming Chaucer Library _Teseida_ (University of Georgia Press). Except for the critical apparatus, however, this edition will have little
interest for Italian studies; Chaucer's copy of the _Teseida_--which the
Chaucer Library edition will attempt to reproduce--was apparently a
corrupt manuscript that lacked important parts of the work and had no
commentary.[3] But research for the Chaucer Library _Teseida_ has provided

---

[1] The Manuscript was first described by G. Vandelli, "Un autografo
della 'Teseide'," _Studi di Filologia Italiana_ 2(1929): 5-76.

[2] For bibliography see VI Centenario della Morte de Giovanni Boccaccio.
Mostra di Manoscritti, Documenti e Edizioni. Firenze-Biblioteca Medicea
Laurenziana. I:Manoscritti e Documenti (Certaldo 1975), p. 33.

[3] See my forthcoming article, "Chaucer, the _Teseida_, and the Visconti
Library at Pavia," _Medium Aevum_.

The *background* orients the reviewer, who probably is unaware of the background of the project; establishes the applicant's mastery of the scholarship of the field.

The point here is to strike a balance: the reviewer must be convinced of the applicant's knowledge of the field and ability to complete the project; but the reviewer must not be overwhelmed with information that would impede the "argument" of the proposal. The proposal should be written both for the specialist and for the nonspecialist.

This paragraph on *previous work* attempts to answer the argument made by a member of the Italian review panel of the same agency regarding an earlier grant proposal. The earlier proposal was for funds to underwrite the Chaucer Library *Teseida* edition. The panel had objected that the edition would not be of significant value for Italian studies. The *Teseida* edition (and its value for Italian and for Chaucerian studies) is brought up here so that the reviewer—again a member of the Italian review panel—will not confuse the two projects and make the same objection.

Detailed information of this sort is more appropriate to *footnotes* than to the body of the text.

an important tool for the project proposed in this grant application--
a complete microfilm collection of the Teseida manuscripts and early
editions. A grant from the City University Research Foundation during
Summer 1974 made possible the purchase of microfilms of the 63 extant
Teseida manuscripts and the editions of 1475, 1490, 1519, and 1528.

Commentaries on the Teseida

   An examination of this material revealed that 18 manuscripts plus
the edition of 1475 contain a commentary on the Teseida. These commentaries can be divided into four groups: 12 manuscripts with
Boccacio's commentary, 4 manuscripts plus the 1475 edition with the
commentary written c. 1425 by Pietro Andrea de' Bassi, and two manuscripts, each with a different anonymous commentary. These are all
listed in the attached appendix.)

   The commentary by Boccaccio is available to scholars in the three
recent editions already mentioned. But since these editions were based
on Boccaccio's holograph, scholars have all but ignored the other 11
manuscripts that contain Boccaccio's commentary. The only study of any
of these manuscripts was an article written some seventy years ago by
Ezio Levi.[4] Levi examined two manuscripts with versions of Boccaccio's
commentary.[5] (Boccaccio's holograph had not been identified in Levi's
time.) He demonstrated that although both manuscripts contained the
same basic commentary, each had significant differences. My own collation of the commentary in five octaves of the poem indicates significant
variants within the manuscript group with Boccaccio's commentary.

   The situation with the manuscripts containing de' Bassi's commentary
is even less fortunate. To my knowledge, no scholars have produced a
comparative study of this group, to note individual differences--and
perhaps other influences--in each commentary. Nor are scholars likely

---

[4]"Adriano de Rossi," Giornale storico della letteratura italiana
55(1910): 237-65.

[5]Aix, Bibl. de la Ville, Cod. 180; Milan. Bibl. Trivulziana. Cod. 1017.

Points out the availability of *microfilmed* materials on which the present proposal is based; indicates that the means are available to achieve the results that the project proposes.

 One paragraph outlines the work to be done; these manuscripts are listed in an *appendix* so as not to impede the "argument" of the proposal.

 Establishes the applicant's knowledge of *previous work* in the field; describes how this project will qualify and differ from previous work.

to examine these differences because de' Bassi's autograph manuscript
has also been identified and edited,[6] being the basis of the 1475 edition of the Teseida. This is unfortunate, because my collation of the
commentary on five octaves of the poem also indicates significant differences within the group with the commentary by de' Bassi.

Besides these published commentaries by Boccaccio and by de' Bassi,
two other commentaries were produced during the 15th century, neither
of which has been published. One (Vatican, Cod. Urbinate lat. 691) follows the traditional method of reproducing the entire Teseida, with commentary interposed. Another, however, (Paris, Bib. Nat., Cod. ital. 581)
is solely a commentary--but one of extraordinary length. This manuscript
comments on only 120 octaves of the Teseida--but for a total of 123 folios.

The Project

The proposed research project would be a descriptive catalogue of
these 18 manuscripts containing commentaries on the Teseida. The catalogue
will describe each manuscript in detail. It will outline and summarize
the contents of each commentary. In describing the 12 manuscripts with
the commentary by Boccaccio and the 4 with the commentary by de' Bassi,
it will detail the variations within each group. The study will also
construct the genealogies of the manuscripts in each of these two groups.

Conclusion

The knowledge of classical myth during the first century of Italian
humanism has all but entirely been credited to Boccaccio's Genealogia
deorum gentilium. The study will provide the basis for reevaluating that
view somewhat by outlining the contents of 18 manuscripts containing
commentaries on the first Italian epic, Boccaccio's Teseida. The study
will describe the variations among the 12 manuscripts with Boccaccio's
commentary and among the 4 manuscripts with de' Bassi's commentary. It
will make available descriptions of two anonymous commentaries that
have never before been edited or described. The project will, finally,
provide scholars with a body of previously unknown information about
the extent of the knowledge of classical myth and literature in the
West during the first century of Italian humanism.

---

[6]Milan, Bibl. Ambrosiana, Cod. D, 534, inf.; in his edition of the
Teseida (1938), Battaglia tentatively identifies this as de' Bassi's
autograph, pp. xxxiii-xxxv, lxxiii-lxxiv.

Describes previously *unpublished* material in the field, which this project will use.

A summary paragraph of the *project,* describing precisely what is to be done and how it is to be done. This and the *concluding paragraph* recap the abstract, which the body of the proposal have been elaborating.

The most important part of the proposal; this argues *why* the project should be funded and lists the specific, important results it will produce.

Appendix:
Commentaries on Boccaccio's Teseida

Editions:

a. with Boccaccio's commentary: ed. Battaglia, Florence 1938; ed. Roncaglia, Bari 1941; ed. Limantani, Milan 1964.

b. with de' Bassi's commentary: printed, Agostino Carnerio. Ferrara 1475. see Hain, Repertorium bibliographicum 3308; Copinger, Supplement to Hain 3308; British Museum, Catalogue of Books Printed in the XVth Century . . . VI; 606-07; Gesamt-katalog der Wiegendrucke 4499.

Manuscripts:

a. Boccaccio's commentary

1. Florence. Bibl. Laurenziana. Cod. Acquisti e Doni 325 (autograph)
2. Aix. Bibl. de la Ville. Cod. 180
3. Florence. Bibl. Laurenziana. Cod. Pluteo XC sup., 140
4. "   .   "   "   . Cod. Ashburnhamiano 963
5. "   .   "   "   . Cod. Rediano 150
6. "   . Bibl. Nazionale . Cod. II. II. 27
7. "   .   "   "   . Cod. Palatino 352, fols. 1-120
8. "   . Bibl. Riccardiana. Cod. 1056
9. Milan   . Bibl. Trivulziana. Cod. 1017
10. Naples   . Bibl. Oratoriana . Cod. Pil., X, 36
11. Rome   . Bibl. Accademia dei Lincei. Cod. 44, B, 12
12. Vatican . Bibl. Apost. Vat . Cod. Chigiano L, VI, 224

b. de' Bassi's Commentary

13. Milan   . Bibl. Ambrosiana . Cod. D, 524, inf. (autograph)
14. Cambridge, Mass. Harvard College Library. Cod. Typ 227 H
15. Chicago . University of Chicago Library. Cod. 541
16. Vatican . Bibl. Apost. Vat . Cod. Vat. lat. 10656

c. anonymous

17. Paris   . Bibl. Nationale . Cod. ital. 581

d. anonymous

18. Vatican . Bibl. Apost. Vat . Cod. Urbinate lat. 691

The appendixes of a research proposal are the appropriate places for technical information that is too detailed or too long to be placed in the "argument" of the grant. The grant writer refers during the body of the grant proposal to the information contained in one or more of the appendixes. Although a list of the manuscripts to be consulted is the proper material for this particular grant proposal, other proposals might contain letters of recommendation and support for the project, samples of the materials to be used in the project, charts, illustrations, statistics, and the like. The appendixes, in other words, contain whatever information illuminates the grant proposal, but which is not properly placed within the body of the proposal.

Sample Project Budget[1]

Project Director: *John Smith*	Duration: *8 months*
Starting Date: 1/1/79	Ending Date: 9/1/79

I. Direct Costs
  A. Personnel:
    1. Project Director: Dr. John Smith
      a. 1/1/76–5/31/79: 40% of time
        yearly salary: $19,500
        $19,500 x 40% x 5/12 months $3250
      b. 6/1/79–8/31/79: 100% of time
        $19,500 x 3/12 months   4875
    2. Research assistant: Barbara Smith[2]
      6/1/79–8/31/79: 13 weeks,
      20 hrs/week @ $4.35/hour   1131
    3. Secretary temporary
      8/3/79–8/31/79: 4 weeks,
      40 hrs/week @ $4.73/hour   756.80 $ 9012.80
  B. Employee Benefits:[3]
    Fringe benefits computed at 27% of
    salaries for items 1(a), 1(b), 2, 3
    27% x $9012.80   2433.46 $ 2433.46
  C. Consultants:
    1. Dr. Robert Roberts, Prof. of Sociology,
      State College.
      4 days @ $100 day   400
    2. Mr. Donald Donaldson, Systems Analyst.
      5 days @ $100/day   500 $ 900
  D. Travel:
    1. Two trips to Rochester, N.Y. for
      observation and interviews.
      Air Fare $110
      6 days @ $32/day 192   302
    2. Six trips to Westbury, L.I. for
      observation and interviews.
      20 miles @ 12¢/mile x 6   15 $ 317
  E. Equipment:
    1. Audiometer   300
    2. Special polaroid camera   100 $ 400
  F. Supplies and Materials:
    1. Project materials
      a. 300 PDQ questionnaires @ 50¢ ea
        300 TAP profiles @ 60¢/ea   330
      b. 600 answer sheets @ 30¢/ea   180
      c. Laboratory supplies   200
    2. Office supplies   100
    3. Typewriter rental   150 $ 960

G. Communications:
   1. Telephone for toll calls to schools
      involved in the project   200
   2. Postage for bulk mailing of
      questionnaires   40 $ 240
H. Services:
   1. Duplication, reproduction,
      Xerox   200
   2. Machine scoring of answer
      sheets by NCS: 600 @ 75¢/ea   450
   3. Data processing and key punch
      30 hours @ $10/hr   300 $ 950
I. Publication Costs: $ 500
J. Other Direct Costs:
   1. Computer Time: 4 hrs @ $150/hr $ 600
K. Subtotal of Direct Costs: $16,413.26
II. Indirect Costs
    Calculated at 58% of salaries and wages
    (58% x 9012.80) $ 5,227.42
III. Total Project Costs $21,630.68

---

[1] This budget was supplied by the Research Foundation of the City University of New York and was based on its document, "Outline for a Model Proposal Budget."

[2] Minimum wages and salaries mandated both by granting agencies and by institutional research foundation vary; it is essential to ascertain these figures correctly. An institutional grants officer should be able to provide help here.

[3] As with salaries, rates and methods for fringe benefits vary. Check with your grants officer.

A DESCRIPTIVE BIBLIOGRAPHY OF PROPOSAL WRITING

General:

Lois De Bakey and Selma De Bakey. "The Art of Persuasion: Logic and Language in Proposal Writing," *Grants Magazine: The Journal of Sponsored Research and Other Programs* 1 (March 1978): 43–60. Argues for the necessity of logic, clarity, accuracy, and coherence in the proposal. A kind of *Elements of Style* for proposal writers, it lists flaws in usage, cliches, jargon, fad words, circumlocutions, and redundancies to avoid, and warns against common errors in grammar and punctuation.

Mary Hall. *Developing Skills in Proposal Writing.* 2d ed. Portland, Ore.: Continuing Education Publications, 1977. $12.50. Excellent and thorough, this is the best general introductory guide to the subject. Especially valuable is the checklist appendix of questions for each stage of the proposal. F. Lee Jacquette and Barbara L. Jacquette. "What Makes a Good Proposal?" Avail. from The Foundation Center, free. Repr. from the January/February 1973 *Foundation News*. Briefly touches the major points of proposal writing, and provides a good checklist of several questions the writer is to answer when reviewing the grant proposal.

Robert A. Mayer. "What Will a Foundation Look for When You Submit a Grant Proposal?" Avail. from The Foundation Center, free. Repr. from the July 1972 *Library Journal*. Suggests ways to prepare a grant proposal, keeping the granting agency's interests and concerns in mind.

Proposal Planning and Proposal Writing. Grantsmanship Center, 1031 S. Grand Ave., Los Angeles, Calif. 90015. $2.45. This excellent booklet is the most widely used general guide and introduction to the subject.

Virginia P. White. *Grants: How to Find Out About Them and What to Do Next*. Plenum: New York, 1975. Contains a three-part section on the grants making process.

For the Professional:

Jean Brodsky, ed. *The Proposal Writer's Swipe File II: 14 Professionally Written Grant Proposals . . . prototypes of approaches, styles, and structures*. Non Profit-Ability Series. Washington, D.C.: Taft Products, 1976. Although it is constructed solely for the professional seeking grants for organizations and institutions, the book is of interest to anyone who wishes to examine professional proposals.

4. In Conclusion

SUPPLEMENTARY GRANTS

One final word: although they tend not to publicize this, many agencies (such as NEH) permit supplementary grant applications. Often, once a project begins the grantee discovers that the costs are greater than anticipated. Often a grant budget falls victim to rising costs and inflation (since it is not uncommon for a year to elapse between the time a budget is submitted and the grant period begins). Those who realize that their budgets are insufficient should consult their granting agencies. The agencies might offer a supplementary grant on the theory that this will insure the results originally projected (instead of producing an insufficient result that is of little value). Some agencies will also supplement a grant originally made by another agency. As was stated before, one should neither underestimate or overestimate one's budget. So, too, when a budget is found to be insufficient, the researcher should inform the agency so that, if nothing else, it can be aware that this might affect the outcome of the project.

IF THE PROPOSAL IS NOT FUNDED

This is a time of increasing sophistication among academics about the availability of grant funds and the methods of securing them. Because of the inevitable competition, the applicant must be prepared to accept a rejection of his or her proposal. The applicant should remember, though, that unlike books and articles, a grant prospectus can be submitted simultaneously to more than one agency. In case of dual funding, an arrangement is worked out whereby the agencies split the budget. (In an ongoing project, the applicant might convince one agency to defer the funding until the following year.)

In the event that the proposal is turned down, the applicant should try to discover the reasons, in order to improve the chances for funding in other applications. The provisions of the Freedom of Information Act obligate the federal government to reveal the reasons why any federal grant proposal was not funded. Private foundations do not have to reveal such information, however. But a courteous request for information for the sake of improving one's future chances will often elicit the reasons. It has been my experience that most agencies will gladly give reviews. If the applicant has been corresponding with someone in the foundation this also makes such information easier to come by. If the applicant resubmits the proposal to the agency at a later date, reference can be made to these reviews, indicating how the suggestions and comments have been incorporated into the revised proposal.

THE RESEARCH GRANT AND THE SCHOLAR'S INCOME TAX

If a research project is funded, the applicant should keep in mind the availability of several income tax benefits for funded research. The income tax laws on academic research are a bit complex, so before beginning the project, the scholar should be aware of those provisions that will provide benefits.

This discussion purposely does not go into great detail. Instead it will identify a few areas which should be studied for possible use by the researcher-taxpayer. One reason for this is that the income tax laws are so complex that any discussion of them must, of necessity, be either very brief or very long. Another reason is that IRS interpretations of tax law provisions affecting scholars often seem conflicting. The agency tends to operate on a case-by-case basis. So one can suggest general guidelines and not much more. For the scholar seriously interested in enjoying the tax benefits earned by doing research, a short bibliography has been included at the end of this section. Since careful attention to taxes can often means the savings of hundreds or even thousands of tax dollars, the scholar should definitely become aware of the information contained in one or more of these publications. One of the best sources of information is the *Tax Guide for College Teachers and Other School Personnel.*

Following are a list of general topics:

Records: the basis of all "successful" income tax returns and all successful income tax audits is a complete and well-kept set of records. Because of my own extensive research expenses, I am audited by the IRS every year. My experience has been that the IRS insists that all claimed research expenses be substantiated. This can sometimes be in the form of a diary (where the researcher might record the round-trip mileage in traveling to a library or the expense of taking another scholar or a member of a research institution to lunch for the purpose of discussing one's work). But it is best to substantiate all research-related expenses with some piece of paper: dinner checks, parking stubs, admission ticket stubs, toll receipts, etc. As researchers, we are used to working with and classifying pieces of paper, so this task should certainly not be difficult—and could save the researcher from unnecessarily overpaying taxes.

Home Office: Previous to 1976, all teachers were allowed to claim a deduction on their tax returns for use of a home office. This was usually a room of one's home and the deduction included a percentage of the depreciation in the teacher's home, plus the cost of the electricity, heating, cleaning, mortgage interest, property taxes, etc., required to maintain that office. In 1976, Congressional legislation required that the home office be the taxpayer's *principal place of business*. This eliminated home offices for teachers, whose principal place of business is not their homes.

A grant recipient may, however, be able to claim home office expenses if it can be proved that part or all of the grant research was conducted at home, i.e., the place where the recipient performed the work which the grant required (the principal place of business) was at home. This would not apply, of course, in cases where one's institution "donated" office space as part of its cost-sharing.

Research Travel: One important area which scholars and educators can use to advantage is that of travel for the purpose of research and study. The point to keep in mind is that study or research must be the principal and organizing purpose of the travel. ("Travel" here can include not only transportation costs, but all costs connected with maintaining oneself away from home.) Many grants include travel funds. But travel expenses beyond the amount in the grant are legitimate tax deductions.

Fellowships and Grants: under certain conditions, scholars may invoke Section 117 (c) of the Internal Revenue Code of 1954. The effect will be to exclude up to $300 per month of the *income* (not the specified items, such as supplies or travel) of a fellowship or grant.

The provisions are these:

1. The grant must not be compensation for past, present, or future services.
2. The grant must not be to pursue research for the benefit of the grantor or granting agency; the primary purpose must, rather, be to further the training of the recipient "in [his or her] individual capacity."

3. Up to $300 per month may be excluded from taxable income.
4. During one's whole career, a total of 36 months (not necessarily consecutive) may be excluded.
5. The grant must be from a government agency or qualifying grant-making organization.
   (*N.B.* All the agencies listed in this book so qualify.)

General things should be kept in mind about the $300 per month exclusion:

1. Although the 36 months need not be consecutive, the researcher is obliged to exclude taxable fellowship income in any month that one is eligible. If one chooses not to exclude, or forgets to, or is unaware of the eligibility to exclude, that month is lost from the lifelong total of 36.
2. If taxable fellowship income during any month is less than $300, the researcher must still exclude the income for the month and subtract the month from the life-long total of 36.
3. Because of the employer-employee relationship and also because they tend to require future services, grants from a researcher's own institution are generally not excludable.
4. There is a possibility that the IRS may extend a recent ruling about graduate student fellowships to postdoctoral fellowships. The ruling was that when an income exclusion was claimed during one tax year, the taxpayer could not income average for the next four years. This should be taken into account when deciding whether to claim an exclusion.

The scholar who is awarded a fellowship or grant should be aware of these few considerations. Beyond this, however, scholars are urged to study works from the following list.

BIBLIOGRAPHY: THE SCHOLAR'S INCOME TAX

Executive Reports Corporation. *Educator's Tax Desk Manual.* Englewood Cliffs, N.J.: Prentice-Hall, 1971.
Maurice C. Greenbaum. "Tax Aspects of Leaves and Travel: Reminders for Professors," *PMLA* 70 (1965): A-6.
Internal Revenue Service. *Tax Information for American Scholars in the U.S. and Abroad.* IRS Publication No. 520. Superintendent of Documents, G.P.O., Washington, D.C. 20402.
Carel Prater. *Teachers' Income Tax Informer.* Augusta, Ga.: National Teachers' Tax Association. Annual.
Tax Guide for College Teachers and Other School Personnel. Washington, D.C.: Academic Information Service, 1973. Annual.
Teachers' Income Tax Guide. Costa Mesa, Calif.: Teachers' Tax Service. Annual.

Appendixes

A   Granting Agencies

The following is a list of agencies whose major commitment is to humanities grants for research and study. Not included are those agencies whose interest in the humanities is marginal or is limited to a specific geographical area. (For a method of identifying such agencies, consult Appendix B on the work of the Foundation Center.)

The list is also not concerned with graduate school fellowships; its purpose is to provide information about research and study opportunities for those who have completed their professional training. Many grant programs are, however, open to a wide variety of applicants. In describing these programs, all those who are eligible to apply are indicated. Unless otherwise noted, these grant programs are open to humanists of any nationality.

Each grant entry is organized in a concise and uniform format. In reading an entry, the grant seeker should first consult the italicized words in the *Conditions* category. These words (*Ph.D., younger faculty, U.S. citizen,* and the like) will immediately indicate the eligibility requirements for the grant program in question. (The occasional abbreviation *ABD* indicates that one of the conditions for a grant is that a graduate student must have completed all requirements for the Ph.D., except the dissertation.)

There are nine categories of information. First, the *name* of the granting agency is provided, followed by the *type* or title of grant, e.g., fellowship, scholarship, grant, grant-in-aid, or Rome Prize Fellowships. Then a summary describing the *purpose* of the program is given: to support research, to finance travel for research in another part of the world, etc. The *number* of grants available annually is provided, as well as the type of *support* (monetary and other) the applicant can expect to receive. The category *conditions* not only sets out the eligibility requirements (as mentioned above) but also when and where the award must be used. This is followed by information on the program's *duration,* e.g., one year, two semesters, a summer, and the *deadline* date for applications to the granting agencies. *Inquiries,* the last category, provides the name, address, and telephone number of the granting agency. It is to this address that correspondence should be sent. Any additional information made available by the granting agency is indicated immediately following the address. This could be in the form of a brochure, an application form, or additional instructions for filing an application.

The information included in this appendix was based on that provided by the granting agencies. When a category is omitted it is an indication that there are no specific criteria. For example, when the deadline category does not appear, this means there is no final date for receipt of application by the agency. Every effort has been made to bring the list up to date. But since grants programs often change conditions, support, and deadlines, prospective applicants should make preliminary inquiries as soon as they identify programs suited to their research interests.

The grants are cross-referenced, in two separate indexes, by subject and by the geographical area where the grant work can take place. The key to each index is the identification number at the beginning of each grant description. The grant list has been arranged alphabetically to facilitate those who wish information about a specific agency.

1. *Name:*   *American Academy in Rome*
   Type: NEH Postdoctoral Fellowships
   Purpose: One year's study and research in the School of Classical Studies at the Academy in Rome. Fields of award include classical studies, post-classical humanistic studies (political, economic, cultural, and church history, history of literature and musicology for the period AD 300 to AD 1800), Italian Studies (including a wide variety of topics), and History of Art.
   Number: At least 4 annually; as many additional awards as resources permit.
   Support: Stipend of $450 a month; travel allowance of $1400; supplies allowance of $400. A single or double bedroom at the Academy or, if accompanied by children, $165 a month rental allowance. One meal daily (except Sundays). A study or studio at the Academy.
   Conditions: Candidates must be *American citizens* of ability and achievement who hold the *doctorate* or are certified to receive it before the fellowship begins. Fellows must be in residence at the Academy during the period of the fellowship. School year runs from early September to 31 August.
   Duration: 1 year.
   Deadline: 15 November. Announcements by about 1 April.
   Inquiries: Executive Secretary
                American Academy in Rome
                41 E. 65th St.
                New York, NY 10021
                212-535-4250
                Brochure and application forms.

2. *Name:*   *American Academy in Rome*
   Type: Rome Prize Fellowships

Purpose: One year's study and research in the School of Classical Studies at the Academy in Rome. Areas include Classical Studies (literature, history, art, and archaeology), Post-Classical Humanistic Studies, Italian Studies (post-doctoral only), History of Art, Byzantine, and Medieval Studies. The Academy also has a School of Fine Arts, which sponsors its own fellowships.

Number: At least 5 annually at the School of Classical Studies; as many additional awards as resources permit.

Support: Stipend of $450 per month; lodgings and study at the Academy. Married fellows with children, who must be housed outside the building, receive an additional $165 per month. Travel allowance ($1400), supplies allowance ($400). One meal daily (except Sunday).

Conditions: *American citizens* of ability and achievement. *ABD* applicants must have completed at least one year's work on dissertation. Fellows must be in residence at the Academy during period of fellowship. School year runs from early September to 31 August.

Deadline: 15 November. Announcements by about 1 April.

Inquiries: Executive Secretary
American Academy in Rome
41 E. 65th St.
New York, NY 10021
212-535-4250
Brochure and application forms.

3. *Name*   *American Antiquarian Society*

Type: Fred Harris Daniels Fellowships

Purpose: Research in Society's collection of resources in early American history and culture.

Number: Varies.

Support: Up to a total of $1800 for one to three months' residence at the Society.

Conditions: Fellowships are open to individuals engaged in scholarly research and writings in early American history and culture, including foreign nationals and persons at work on doctoral dissertations. Grants will be made only to those residing more than 50 miles from Worcester, Mass.

Deadline: 1 February. Announcement 15 March.

Inquiries: John B. Hench, Research and Publication Officer
American Antiquarian Society
185 Salisbury St.
Worcester, MA 01609
617-755-5221
Further information available each fall.

4. *Name:*   *American Antiquarian Society*

Type: NEH Fellowships
Purpose: Research in Society's collection of resources in early American history and culture.
Number: 2.
Support: Up to $1666 per month for 6 to 12 months' residence at the Society.
Conditions: Fellows must be *U.S. citizens* or *residents* for at least 3 years. Fellowships may not be awarded to degree candidates or for study leading to advanced degrees. Fellows must devote full-time to research at the Society and may not undertake teaching or any other major activities. They may not hold other grants, except sabbatical or other grants from their own institution.
Deadline: 1 February. Announcement 15 March.
Inquiries: John B. Hench, Research and Publication Officer
American Antiquarian Society
185 Salisbury St.
Worcester, MA 01609
617-755-5221
Further information available each fall.

5. *Name:* *American Association of University Women Educational Foundation* (AAUW)
Type: American Fellowships
Purpose: Dissertation and postdoctoral research.
Number: 70 annually.
Support: $3500 to $7000; up to $9000 for postdoctoral fellowships.
Conditions: Applicants must be *women, U.S. citizens,* or *permanent residents.* Dissertation fellowship candidates must be *ABD* by 2 January preceding commencement of fellowship. "Great importance is attached to the project on which the applicant wishes to work, its probable significance to knowledge, and the applicant's qualifications to pursue it." Fellow must devote full time to project. For postdoctoral competition, preference is given to those with junior academic appointments and who plan to use the fellowship year for research leave. Preference is also given to women whose professional careers have been interrupted. Program does not provide funds for equipment, publication subsidies, travel grants, tuition, or funds to repay loans.
Duration: 1 July–30 June.
Deadline: 15 December. 15 April notification.
Inquiries: AAUW Educational Foundation Programs Office
2401 Virginia Ave., N.W.
Washington, DC 20037
202-785-7700
Announcement.

6. *Name:*   *American Association of University Women-International Fellowship of University Women* (AAUW-IFUW)
Type: International fellowships
Purpose: Graduate study or advanced research in any field in any country other than the Fellow's own.
Number: 6 (for research anywhere); 35 (for research in U.S.).
Support: Varies according to cost of living at place of study.
Conditions: Applicants must be *women* who are citizens of countries other than the United States and members of an IFUW organization. Applicants must present a plan of study or research which will advance their professional competence. Applicant must intend to return home to pursue her professional career. Preference will be given to applicants with specific positions to return to in their own countries.
Duration: 1 academic year beginning in September (not renewable).
Deadline: 1 December. 15 March notification.
Inquiries: AAUW Educational Foundation Program Office
2401 Virginia Ave., N.W.
Washington, DC 20037
202-785-7700
Announcement.

7. *Name:*   *American Council of Learned Societies* (ACLS)
Type: Fellowship Program
Purpose: To allow free time for research in the humanities and in the social sciences (if the project has a predominately humanistic emphasis).
Support: Up to $13,500. Can include salary, travel, clerical and research assistance, support of dependents.
Conditions: *Ph.D* or equivalent. Degree to have been awarded before January 1978 (for 1980 competition); not more than 51 years old as of deadline (except in extraordinary circumstances). ACLS permits recipients to use awards any time within a 1½ year period from July 1 following award notification. Fellows must be able to devote six continuous months to full-time research.
Duration: 6 to 12 months of continuing study.
Deadline: 30 September. Announcements within four months.
Inquiries: ACLS, Office of Fellowships and Grants
800 Third Ave.
New York, NY 10022
212-223-1164
Brochure: *Aids to Individual Scholars.*

8. *Name:*   *American Council of Learned Societies* (ACLS)
Type: Grants for Research on Chinese Civilization

Purpose: To facilitate postdoctoral research on Chinese civilization up to 1911, either in this country or abroad. To aid
experienced scholars in projects which produce a mature
overview of a given problem, age, or field of knowledge.

Support: Up to $15,000 (but the majority are smaller).

Conditions: *U.S. citizens* and permanent residents; *Ph.D* or its equivalent. Funds are for research-related domestic or foreign
travel, research costs and maintenance for short periods.
Funds may supplement sabbatical salaries and other
grants. Support not given for straight translation projects.
Cost of travel to Asia for less than 6 months' field research cannot be defrayed. Preference given to scholars
who have not had substantial research support within
past 5 years.

Duration: At least 6 months of uninterrupted research.

Deadline: 1 December. Announcements within 4 months.

Inquiries: ACLS, Office of Fellowships and Grants
800 Third Ave.
New York, NY 10022
212-223-1164
Brochure: *Aids to Individual Scholars.*

9. *Name:*   *American Council of Learned Societies* (ACLS)

Type: Grants in Aid

Purpose: To provide funds in support of significant humanistic
research.

Support: Up to $3,000.

Conditions: *U.S. or Canadian citizen; Ph.D.* or equivalent. Grants
"to be used exclusively to advance specific programs of
research in progress by contributing to the scholar's
essential personal expenses for that purpose." Expenses
may include travel and maintenance away from home,
research or clerical assistance, reproduction or purchase
of materials, but not living expenses at home.

Deadline: 15 December. Announcements within 4 months.

Inquiries: ACLS, Office of Fellowships and Grants
800 Third Ave.
New York, NY 10022
212-223-1164
Brochure: *Aids to Individual Scholars.*

10. *Name:*   *American Council of Learned Societies* (ACLS)

Type: Mellon Fellowships for Chinese Studies

Purpose: "To sustain and advance the competence of scholars
trained in the area of historical or contemporary Chinese
studies, by providing opportunities to maintain and improve research and teaching skills."

Support: Up to $15,000, depending on length of tenure.
Conditions: *Ph.D.; American or Canadian citizens* and permanent residents. Awards are to further specialization in the field of previous training, for the acquisition of new methodological skills, and for advanced language training in Japanese and classical and modern Chinese. Study is to be on the advanced level. Recognition is given to needs of scholars who work at a distance from major centers of Chinese studies. Research may be undertaken during grant period, but this is not to be applicant's prime objective. Preference to untenured scholars with at least 3 years' teaching experience.
Duration: Minimum of 1 semester or 2 quarters (for advanced study and research at major university centers) or minimum of 6 months (for advanced language study and research at a language teaching center in East Asia).
Deadline: 1 December. Announcements within 4 months.
Inquiries: ACLS, Office of Fellowships and Grants
800 Third Ave.
New York, NY 10022
212-223-1164
Brochure: *Aids to Individual Scholars.*

11. *Name:* *American Council of Learned Societies* (ACLS)
Type: Research Fellowships for Recent Recipients of the Ph.D.
Purpose: To support significant humanities research.
Support: Up to $7,000.
Conditions: Scholars whose *Ph.D.* degrees were awarded since January 1, 1978 (for 1980 competition). ACLS permits recipients to use awards any time within a 1½ year period from 1 July following award notification. Although primarily to provide free time, amounts from grants may support travel, clerical or research assistance, or reproduction or purchase of materials.
Duration: 1 semester or 4½ months.
Deadline: 30 September. Announcements within four months.
Inquiries: ACLS, Office of Fellowships and Grants
800 Third Ave.
New York, NY 10022
212-223-1164
Brochure: *Aids to Individual Scholars.*

12. *Name:* *American Council of Learned Societies* (ACLS)
Type: Research Grants for East European Studies
Purpose: Postdoctoral grants for research in the social sciences or humanities relating to Albania, Bulgaria, Czechoslovakia, Hungary, Poland, Romania, Yugoslavia, East Germany since 1945, and to modern Greece. Research related to Finland and the Baltic States (only if they have rele-

	vance to non-Soviet Eastern Europe).

Support: Up to $10,000.

Conditions: *Ph.D.* Program particularly invites comparative research on social institutions and processes; program also supports "research of conceptual and theoretical focus and manifest disciplinary relevance, empirically based on immigrant groups on communities from Eastern Europe." Small grants (for research-related domestic or foreign travel for short periods), summer stipends (in exceptional cases), larger grants (up to $10,000) for at least 6 months' uninterrupted research. Grants may supplement sabbatical funds and other grants. Foreign travel grants only in exceptional circumstances.

Duration: Short periods or at least 6 months (depending on stipend).

Deadline: 1 December. Announcement within 4 months.

Inquiries: ACLS, Office of Fellowships and Grants
800 Third Ave.
New York, NY 10022
212-223-1164
Brochure: *Aids to Individual Scholars.*

13. *Name:* *American Council of Learned Societies* (ACLS)
Type: Study Fellowships
Purpose: To aid younger scholars (normally under 36) in the humanities to enlarge their range of knowledge by study in a discipline other than their own, one which normally employs a different methodology. (Social and natural scientists wishing to study a humanistic discipline are also eligible.)

Support: Up to $12,000.

Conditions: Younger candidates with a few years' teaching since earning the *Ph.D.* ACLS permits recipients to use awards any time within a 1½ year period from 1 July following award notification. Recipients must "take advantage of specific educational opportunities . . . within a structured program or under appropriate senior professors."

Duration: 6 to 12 months of continuous study.

Deadline: 15 November. Announcements within four months.

Inquiries: ACLS, Office of Fellowships and Grants
800 Third Ave.
New York, NY 10022
212-223-1164
Brochure: *Aids to Individual Scholars.*

14. *Name:* *American Council of Learned Societies* (ACLS)
Type: Travel Grants for Humanists to International Meetings Abroad.

Purpose:	To enable humanists to participate in international scholarly congresses and conferences held outside North America (including the Caribbean).
Support:	Grants cover only air-fare on U.S. flag carriers and are paid after the meeting.
Conditions:	*U.S. citizens* or permanent residents. Only those who read papers or take some active official part in the meeting are eligible. *Ph.D.* or its equivalent. Meetings having to do with education or pedagogy, journalism or communications research or development, or the creative or performing arts are not eligible. In addition to humanists, social scientists and legal scholars who specialize in the history or philosophy of their disciplines may apply if the meeting they wish to attend is so oriented. Applicants may not have received an ACLS travel grant during either of the two preceding calendar years. Recommendations for funding must be made by one of the constituent societies of the ACLS (but membership is not required).
Deadline:	1 July for meetings November–February. 1 November for meetings March–June. 1 March for meeting July–October. Announcements within 2 months. Letter stating name, dates, place, and sponsorship of meeting, as well as a brief description of applicant's scholarly interests, and proposed role in the meeting to:
Inquiries:	ACLS, Travel Grant Office 800 Third Ave. New York, NY 10022 212-223-1164 Brochure: *Aids to Individual Scholars.*

15. *Name:* American Institute of Indian Studies
    Type: Postdoctoral study tours in India.

Purpose:	To allow recent Ph.D.s who have not been to India the opportunity to visit persons and institutions of interest.
Support:	$2000.
Conditions:	Recent *Ph.D* from a university which is a member of the Institute or who is currently on the staff of a member institution. Primary field of study and teaching must be South Asia, but applicant may not have yet visited India.
Deadline:	1 to 15 October.
Inquiries:	American Institute of Indian Studies Foster Hall, University of Chicago 1130 E. 59 St. Chicago, IL 60637 312-753-1234

16. *Name:*   *American Institute of Indian Studies*
    Type: Senior Research Fellowships in India
    Purpose: To allow academic specialists in Indian studies a period of research in residence at an Indian university.
    Support: Varies.
    Conditions: *Ph.D* or equivalent. Applicants must be engaged in teaching and/or research at an American institution. Fellows must affiliate themselves with an Indian university.
    Duration: 3 months to 1 year.
    Deadline: 1 to 15 October.
    Inquiries: American Institute of Indian Studies
    Foster Hall, University of Chicago
    1130 E. 59 St.
    Chicago, IL 60637
    312-753-1234

17. *Name:*   *American Institute of Indian Studies*
    Type: Travel grants to India
    Purpose: To aid scholars to travel to India for scholarly purposes.
    Support: Varies.
    Conditions: *Scholars.* Purpose of trip must be for scholarly purposes. Applicant must have a degree from a university that is a member of the Institute or currently be on the staff of a member institution. Grants are only for travel—applicants must secure their own funds for the project which will occupy them in India.
    Deadline: 1 to 15 October.
    Inquiries: American Institute of Indian Studies
    Foster Hall, University of Chicago
    1130 E. 59 St.
    Chicago, IL 60637
    312-753-1234

18. *Name:*   *American Institute of Pakistan Studies* (Villanova University)
    Type: Fellowships
    Purpose: To support *scholars* and advanced graduate students engaged in research on Pakistan in all fields of the humanities and social sciences, particularly in comparative research on Pakistan and other Muslim countries.
    Deadline: 1 January.
    Inquiries: Director
    American Institute of Pakistan Studies
    138 Tolentine Hall, Villanova University
    Villanova, PA 19085
    215-527-2100

19. *Name:*   *American Numismatic Society*
    Type: Grants-in-aid to attend the Society's summer session in numismatics in New York
    Number: 10 annually.
    Support: $750 stipend.
    Conditions: Applicants must be *students* who will have completed at least one year's graduate study in classics, archaeology, history, economic history, or related disciplines. Applications will also be accepted from *junior university or college instructors* with a degree in one of these fields. All applicants must be affiliated with a college or university in the United States or Canada.
    Duration: 9 weeks, mid-June to mid-August.
    Deadline: 1 March. Announcements by 1 April.
    Inquiries: American Numismatic Society
    Broadway & 156 St.
    New York, NY 10032
    212-234-3130
    Announcement.

20. *Name:*   *American Philosophical Society*
    Type: Grants
    Purpose: To support basic research by individuals in all fields of learning.
    Support: Up to $2,000 ($1,000 for active full professors); grants average $1,000.
    Conditions: Applicants must have a *doctoral degree* or equivalent research experience. Grants are to contribute to research costs, travel ($15 per day), supplies, and incidental expenses. Grants are usually to *U.S. citizens,* only to foreign scholars when proposed research deals with American questions. Grants will not be made for salaries, publication subsidies, permanent equipment, travel to meetings, family expenses, conference and symposia expenses, manuscript preparation costs, preparation of bibliographies, concordances and the like, performing arts, creative work in the fine arts, subsistence in lieu of summer teaching, or for training.
    Deadline: Committee on Research meets five times yearly: the first Friday of February, April, June, October, and December. Applications must be received 8 weeks in advance of the meeting at which they are to be considered.
    √ *Inquiries:*   Preliminary letter of inquiry containing informal (one page) project description to be addressed to:
    George W. Corner, Chairman
    Committee on Research, American Philosophical Society
    104 S. 5th St.
    Philadelphia, PA 19106
    215-627-0706
    Announcement.

21. *Name:*   *American Research Institute in Turkey*
    Type: Fellowships
    Purpose: Research and study in Turkey only in any field of humanities and social sciences.
    Support: Maintenance, travel to and from Turkey, travel within Turkey: $500 to $7800 (amount varies according to research needs).
    Conditions: Students (*ABD*) and *scholars* associated with research or educational institutions in U.S. and Canada. Applicant must be engaged in research in any field of the humanities and social sciences (ancient, medieval, and modern) that must be carried out in Turkey.
    Duration: Up to 12 months.
    Deadline: 15 November. Announcements 31 December.
    Inquiries: American Research Institute in Turkey
                 c/o University Museum
                 33rd & Spruce Sts.
                 Philadelphia, PA 19104
                 215-243-4000
                 Announcement and information form available from August on.

22. *Name:*   *American-Scandinavian Foundation*
    Type: Fellowship and grants program
    Purpose: Unrestricted study in the Scandinavian countries: Finland, Iceland, Denmark, Norway, Sweden.
    Number: About 20–25 annually.
    Support: $500 to $6000.
    Conditions: *American citizen* under age 40 with a B.A. degree. Candidates must have a superior record and present a well-defined program of study or research. Language competency required. "Award policies tend to favor assisting younger scholars in reaching degree objectives, but outstanding proposals from all sources are encouraged and will be carefully considered." Interviews at ASF Headquarters are encouraged. All applications must be accompanied by a nonrefundable $10 service fee.
    Duration: Short term to 1 year.
    Deadline: 1 November.
    Inquiries: American-Scandinavian Foundation, Exchange Division
                 127 E. 73 St.
                 New York, NY 10021
                 212-879-9779
                 Application forms and new award announcements are available early each fall.

23. *Name:*   *Archaeological Institute of America*
    Type: Olivia James Traveling Fellowship

Purpose:	For study of classics, sculpture, architecture, archaeology, or history in Greece, the Aegean Islands, Sicily, Southern Italy, Asia Minor, or Mesopotamia.
Number:	1 or more annually.
Support:	Minimum of $5,500, depending on the number of grants.
Conditions:	*U.S. resident.* Individual research project must require travel to Mediterranean or Asia Minor. Report required at end of Fellowship.
Duration:	1 academic year.
Deadline:	31 January. Announcement by 1 April.
Inquiries:	Archaeological Institute of America 53 Park Place, Rm. 802 New York, NY 10007 212-732-6677 Application form available in September.

24. | | |
|---|---|
| *Name:* | *Archaeological Institute of America* |
| *Type:* | Harriet Pomerance Fellowship |
| *Purpose:* | For an individual project in Aegean or Bronze Age archaeology. |
| *Number:* | 1 annually. |
| *Support:* | $1750. |
| *Conditions:* | *U.S. or Canadian resident.* Preference given to candidates whose project requires travel to the Mediterranean. Report required at end of Fellowship. |
| *Duration:* | 1 academic year. |
| *Deadline:* | 31 January. Announcement 1 April. |
| *Inquiries:* | Archaeological Institute of America
53 Park Place, Rm. 802
New York, NY 10007
212-732-6677
Application form available in September. |

25. | | |
|---|---|
| *Name:* | *Atran Foundation* |
| *Type:* | Grants |
| *Purpose:* | To support research in economics, sociology, labor relations, art, science and (Jewish) language and literature. The Foundation also subvents publications in these fields. |
| *Inquiries:* | Atran Foundation
205 W 54th St.
New York, NY 10019
212-245-4610 |

26. | | |
|---|---|
| *Name:* | *Austrian Government Grants* |
| *Type:* | Study, research, and travel grants |
| *Purpose:* | To enable *American teachers* and *students* of German to further their schooling or research projects at Austrian |

	universities and other institutions.
Support:	a. For undergraduates, nine monthly installments of 5,000 Austrian schillings.
	b. For doctoral candidates, nine monthly installments of AS 5,500.
	c. For professors, nine monthly installments of AS 6,500. Also included are health and accident insurance, free tuition at universities, and a travel allowance of AS 2,500 for trips within Austria. Funds for overseas transportation may be obtained through a Fulbright Travel Grant. (*N.B.* Deadline for Fulbright Travel Grant program is 1 February.)
Conditions:	Applicants must be between 20 and 35 years old, with an excellent command of German. *Students* must have completed two years of satisfactory work at a college or university. *Graduates* must continue their studies and/ or research in German language or literature. Applicants must submit a resume, in German, at least two letters of recommendation, detailed description of any study project to be undertaken, plus copies of transcript.
Duration:	9 months, beginning in October.
Deadline:	15 January. Those chosen to submit applications will be notified during the first week of February.
Inquiries:	Austrian Institute
	11 E. 52nd St.
	New York, NY 10022
	Attn: ACSAL Grant
	212-759-5165
	Announcement. Book, *Study in Austria.*
	For information on Fulbright Travel Awards contact:
	Institute of International Education
	809 United Nations Plaza
	New York, NY 10017
	212-883-8200

27. *Name:*	*Axe-Houghton Foundation*
Type:	Grants
Purpose:	To foster and encourage the improvement of language in all its manifestations: remedial speech, public speaking, speaking as an art form (drama, opera, choral work), as well as the written language.
Support:	Varies; average $11,000 (mostly to institutions).
Inquiries:	Axe-Houghton Foundation
	299 Park Ave., 31st fl.
	New York, NY 10001
	212-732-6400

28. *Name:*	*Business and Professional Women's Foundation*

Type: BPW Foundation Research Grant programs; Lena Lake Forrest Fellowship

Purpose: To support research on economic, educational, political, psychological or social factors affecting working women.

Number: 2 to 3 annually.

Support: $500 to $3000.

Conditions: *Doctoral candidates* or *postdoctoral scholars*. Foundation is particularly interested in research "which holds promise for action programs and practical solutions." Major areas of concern include:
1. Development of women's potential for management in education, government, business, and industry.
2. Encouragement of women in nontraditional career choices.
3. Increased participation of women in political life and community action.

Applicants must send a brief description of their proposed projects when requesting application form.

Deadline: 1 January.

Inquiries: Business and Professional Women's Foundation
2012 Massachusetts Ave., N.W.
Washintgon, DC 20036
202-293-1200
Information and application form available in the fall.

29. *Name:* The Mary Ingraham Bunting Institute of Radcliffe College

Type: Bunting Fellowships

Purpose: "To provide the opportunity and support for a professional woman to complete a substantial project in her field and thereby to advance her career." Fellowship holders pursue independent study in academic or professional fields, in creative writing, or in the arts.

Support: Fellowships include office or studio space, auditing privileges, and access to the libraries and other resources of Radcliffe College and Harvard University. Fellowships are in two categories: those with stipend (currently $12,500 a year) and those without stipend (to women recipients of grants from national foundations who are invited to apply to the Institute after the announcement of their fellowships).

Conditions: Applicants must be *women* who have received their *doctorates* by 30 June of the year preceeding application (e.g., by 30 June 1979 for applications with a 15 October 1980 deadline). Fellows may be at any level of career development—from early postdoctoral or its equivalent to senior professional ranks. Appointments are full-time and require residence in the Boston area.

Duration: 1 year: 1 July to 30 June. Renewable after five years.
Deadline: 15 October. Announcement in May.
Inquiries: The Bunting Institute, Radcliffe College
3 James St.
Cambridge, MA 02138
617-495-8214
Brochure.

30. *Name:*   The Mary Ingraham Bunting Institute of Radcliffe College
Type: Independent Educational Studies Project
(funded by National Institute of Education)
Purpose: "To assist qualified faculty members from colleges and universities where teaching is the primary institutional mission to engage in educational research at Radcliffe College for three months during the summer."
Support: $4,500 stipend and $500 research expenses, office space, access to the libraries and other facilities of Radcliffe College and Harvard University.
Conditions: For studies pertaining to education in the social sciences and humanities. "Priority will be given to those studies which reflect the perspectives of women and minorities on various educational issues." Men or women may apply (but Institute will ensure that a significant proportion of the researchers are minority persons and women). Appointees reside in Boston area during fellowship term.
Duration: 3 months, beginning 1 July.
Deadline: 30 October.
Inquiries: The Bunting Institute, Radcliffe College
3 James St.
Cambridge, MA 02138
617-495-8214
Announcement.

31. *Name:*   The Mary Ingraham Bunting Institute of Radcliffe College
Type: Nontenured women faculty fellowships
Purpose: "To provide the opportunity for junior faculty women at major research universities throughout the country to work on projects that promise to make a significant contribution to their fields and to enhance their opportunities for tenure."
Support: $15,000 stipend (for total fellowship period), $3,000 research expenses, up to $1,000 travel expenses (for a trip between home and Cambridge each year during term of appointment), office space. Auditing privileges and access to the libraries and other facilities of Radcliffe College and Harvard University.

Conditions:	Nontenured *women* teaching at a college or university. Residence in Boston area required during fellowship term. Applicants may be nominated by their institutions or may apply directly to the Institute.
Duration:	Either part-time for two years (with one semester of each year at the Institute) or full-time for one year, to be determined by the appointee and her institution.
Deadline:	15 October (for institutional nominations). 15 November (for independent applications). Announcement in May.
Inquiries:	The Bunting Institute, Radcliffe College 3 James St. Cambridge, MA 02138 617-495-8214 Announcement.

32. *Name:*   *Camargo Foundation*

Type:	"Facilities" fellowship for residence at study center in Cassis, France
Purpose:	To facilitate research projects in French culture (particularly Provençal language and literature). Center also offers residence to artists and musicians.
Number:	10 annually.
Support:	Provides apartments and reference library; a few stipends for junior fellows not on salary.
Conditions:	University, college, secondary school *faculty* or graduate *students* (*ABD*, recommended by department chairman or thesis advisors who have approved their projects). Selection of scholars is based on a review of their proposed projects and of their scholarly activity. Research should be at an advanced stage, not requiring resources unavailable in Aix-Cassis-Marseilles.
Duration:	1 or 2 academic semesters.
Deadline:	1 March. Announcements 15 April.
Inquiries:	Director La Foundation Camargo 13260, Cassis, France Tele: 91-01-83-11; 91-01-81-57 *or* Mrs. Jane M. Viggiani Main St. East Haddem, CT 06423 203-873-8292 Application form and memorandum to Camargo candidates.

33. *Name:*   *Canadian Federation for the Humanities*

Type:	Publication grants

Purpose: To aid publication of completed scholarly manuscripts in the humanities (ancient and modern languages and literatures, philosophy, history, fine arts, musicology, archaeology, and religious studies).
Number: About 110 annually.
Support: Varies.
Conditions: Applicants must be *Canadian scholars* or *Canadian publishers.* Manuscripts are to be in the humanities (as described above). Ineligible are textbooks, anthologies, unrevised theses, fiction, and poetry, incomplete manuscripts, and manuscripts which have reached galley proof stage.
Inquiries: Publications Programme
Canadian Federation for the Humanities
151 Slater St.
Ottawa, Ontario
Canada KIP 5H3
613-238-6112

34. *Name:* *Center for Field Research*
Type: Grants and volunteer support
Purpose: To aid scientists and humanists conducting field research. Center provides funds and volunteer staff recruited by Earthwatch, a national volunteer organization. Projects are to improve the public's understanding of science.
Support: Volunteer staff plus awards from $1,500 to $50,000, depending on number of volunteers involved.
Conditions: Center favors research directed by *Ph.D.s.* Dissertation projects and undergraduate research are not eligible. No limits on geographic location of projects. Volunteers are generally available from 2 to 4 week periods, long field seasons may be supported by a succession of teams. Eligible disciplines in the humanities include, but are not limited to: anthropology, archaeology, art history, cartography, conservation, ethology, folklore, historic preservation, and musicology.
Duration: Varies according to project.
Deadline: Preliminary proposals at any time. Formal proposals will be requested by Center. These must precede field work by 9 months. Selection committee meets 15 May and 1 October.
Inquiries: Elizabeth E. Caney, Director of Research
The Center for Field Research
10 Juniper Rd.
Box 127-B
Belmont, MA 02178
617-489-3032
Announcement, application brochure, and copy of *Earthwatch Research Expeditions.*

35. *Name:*   *Center for Hellenic Studies* (Trustees for Harvard University)
Type: Fellowships for individual study and research
Purpose: To give scholars from around the world the opportunity to work on a significant project in the field of ancient Greek literature, history, or philosophy.
Number: 8 annually.
Support: Stipend of $9000. Housing (including utilities), study, use of library, and other facilities of Center.
Duration: 1 academic year.
Conditions: Applicants must be "qualified members of the profession" (in American terms, *postdoctoral*), between the ages of 25 and 40 (these limits are flexible in special cases).
Deadline: 31 October.
Inquiries: The Director
Center for Hellenic Studies
3100 Whitehaven St., N.W.
Washington, DC 20008
202-234-3738
Announcement and application forms.

36. *Name:*   *William Andrews Clark Memorial Library* (University of California, Los Angeles)
Type: Andrew W. Mellon Fellowships
Purpose: Advanced postdoctoral research at the Library in subjects relevant to its collections and interests (17–18th century England, especially Age of Dryden; Oscar Wilde and the 1890s; Montana history; modern fine printing. See *Dictionary Catalogue of the William Andrews Clark Memorial Library,* 15 vols. Boston: Hall, 1973).
Number: Varies.
Support: Stipends average $500 per month.
Conditions: Applicants must have *Ph.D.* or equivalent and be engaged in advanced study and research. Preference given to applicants from outside Southern California. Fellowships are held in residence at the Library.
Duration: 1 to 4 months, during the regular academic year or the summer.
Deadline: 10 October; 25 March.
Inquiries: Director
William Andrews Clark Memorial Library
2520 Cimarron St.
Los Angeles, CA 90018
213-731-8529
Announcement.

37. *Name:*   *William Andrews Clark Memorial Library* (University of California, Los Angeles)

Type: Postdoctoral summer research fellowship
Purpose: Research at the Library in subjects relevant to its collections and interests. Fellow's project is conducted in relation to a study program conducted each summer. 1979 topic was "Between Drake and Cook: English Maritime Enterprise in the Seventeenth and First Half of the Eighteenth Centuries."
Number: 6 annually.
Support: $1500, plus travel allowance within continental United States.
Conditions: Candidates must have had the *Ph.D.* for not more than five years. Fellowships are held in residence at the Library.
Duration: 6 week summer period.
Deadline: 22 January.
Inquiries: Director
William Andrews Clark Memorial Library
2520 Cimarron St.
Los Angeles, CA 90018
213-731-8529
Announcement.

38. *Name:* *College Art Association*
Type: Millard Meiss Publication Fund grants
Purpose: To subsidize publication costs of book-length scholarly manuscripts in art history which cannot be published without a subsidy.
Support: Less than the total costs of production.
Conditions: Awards are open to *scholars* of any nation. Manuscripts (in art history) must already have been accepted by a publisher. Commercial or university presses are eligible. Publisher must submit a written statement giving technical specifications of the proposed publication, stating the amount of subsidy required, and enclosing all reviews of the manuscript that have been submitted. Applicants must be members of the College Art Association. Author must agree to relinquish all claims to royalties until such earnings here reached the amount of the subsidy. Publications in all periods of art history are eligible, but fund will not subsidize museum catalogs or excavation reports.
Deadline: 1 March (for Spring meeting of Meiss Fund committee).
1 September (for Fall meeting of Meiss Fund committee).
Inquiries: College Art Association of America
16 E. 52nd St.
New York, NY 10022
212-755-3532
Announcement and application forms.

39. *Name:*   *Council for International Exchange of Scholars*
    Type: Fulbright-Hays Postdoctoral Awards
    Purpose: University lecturing and postdoctoral research abroad.
    Number: About 500 annually: about 50 in American literature and civilization, 40 in linguistics and teaching English as a second language, a few in other modern languages and literatures.
    Support: Stipend that varies (in local currency or in a combination of local currency and dollars). Round-trip transportation for the grantee and sometimes one dependent. Maintenance for the grantee and dependents. Allowance for essential incidental expenses. Supplemental dollar grant to lecturers in certain Asian, African, and Latin American countries.
    Conditions: *U.S. citizens.* For lecturers: college teaching experience; for research: doctoral degree or equivalent. In some cases, knowledge of host country language.
    Duration: 1 academic year (some for shorter periods).
    Deadline: 12 to 18 months in advance.
1 June: American Republics, Australia, and New Zealand.
1 July: Asia, Africa, and Europe.
Late opportunities are sometimes available.
    Inquiries: Council for International Exchange of Scholars
Conference Board of Associated Research Councils
11 Dupont Circle, N.W., Suite 300
Washington, DC 20036
202-833-4950
Registration form. Announcements will be sent for next two years.

40. *Name:*   *The Shelby Cullom Davis Center for Historical Studies* (Princeton University)
    Type: Research fellowships
    Purpose: To pursue individual research and to contribute actively to the weekly seminar of the Davis Center.
    Support: One-half annual academic salary (up to $17,000). $1,500 transportation costs. $500 research expenses per semester. Certain computer costs.
    Conditions: *Ph.D.,* for highly recommended *younger scholars* (with at least one year's teaching experience) as well as for *senior scholars* with established reputations. Residence in Princeton in order to participate in seminar. Seminar topic for 1980–82 is the relationship between political power and ideology.
    Duration: 1 or 2 semesters (September to January and February to June).
    Deadline: 1 December.
    Inquiries: Secretary

Davis Center for Historical Studies
129 Dickinson Hall
Princeton University
Princeton, NJ 08540
609-452-3000
Announcement.

41. **Name:** *Gladys Krieble Delmas Foundation*
    Type: Fellowships for Venetian Research
    Purpose: To underwrite research in Venice, Italy in several areas
    of study: the history of Venice, the former Venetian
    empire in its various aspects (art, architecture, archae-
    ology, theater, music, literature, natural science, political
    science, economics, the law), contemporary Venetian
    environment (ecology, oceanography, urban planning,
    rehabilitation).
    Number: Varies; 13 in 1979–80 competition.
    Support: Varies. Total support is $40,000 per year. Applications
    may be from $500 to a maximum of $10,000 (for a full
    academic year). Subvention grants available for publica-
    tion of studies resulting from these grants.
    Conditions: For pre-doctoral and postdoctoral research in Venice.
    Applicants must be *U.S. citizens,* experienced in research.
    If graduate students, they must be *ABD.*
    Deadline: 15 January. Announcement 1 April.
    Inquiries: The Gladys Krieble Delmas Foundation
    40 Wall St.
    New York, NY 10006
    No telephone.
    Announcement and instruction sheet.

42. **Name:** *Henry L. and Grace Doherty Foundation*
    Type: Fellowships in social sciences
    Purpose: Advanced study in Latin America for *U.S. citizens* under
    40 with no previous Latin American experience.
    Inquiries: Doherty Fellowship Committee
    Program in Latin American Studies
    Princeton University
    240 E. Pyne
    Princeton, NJ 08540
    609-452-3000

43. **Name:** *Charles R. Drew National Scholarship Commission*
    Type: Creative and Research Fellowships
    Support: Up to $1,000.
    Conditions: Applicants must be *U.S. citizens.* Humanities grants are
    offered in three areas: creative work (fiction, poetry,

drama, biography, and the essay), scholarly work, and research (methods, history, and techniques of education on all levels).

Deadline: 30 November.
Inquiries: Charles R. Drew National Scholarship Commission
Omega Psi Phi Fraternity
2714 Georgia Ave., N.W.
Washington, DC 20001
202-667-7158

44. *Name:* *Dublin Institute of Advanced Studies*
Type: Scholarship to the School of Celtic Studies
Purpose: Celtic studies at the Institute.
Number: 6 annually.
Support: Varies.
Duration: 1 year; possible extention for another year.
Deadline: 31 March.
Inquiries: Miss Patricia O'Neil, Registrar
School of Celtic Studies
Dublin Institute of Advanced Studies
10 Burlington Rd.
Dublin 4, Ireland

45. *Name:* *Dumbarton Oaks Center for Byzantine Studies*
Trustees for Harvard University
Type: Fellowships
Purpose: Research in Byzantine Civilization in all its aspects, including realtions with neighboring cultures. Fields include the late Roman and early Christian period, and the Middle Ages generally. Comparative studies of Byzantine cultural exchanges with the Latin West and with Slavic countries are encouraged. Fellowships are offered in art history, archaeology, philology, architecture, history, law, music, theology, philosophy, and other disciplines.
Support: *Junior fellowships* (dissertation year fellowship): $5000, plus housing and partial board; *visiting fellowships* (faculty and established *scholars*): $7000 minimum, plus housing and partial board.
Duration: 1 academic year at the Center (October to June). In exceptional cases for shorter periods. Reappointment not normally made within less than five years.
Deadline: 15 December.
Announcement by 15 February.
Inquiries: The Assistant Director
Dumbarton Oaks
1703 32 St., N.W.
Washington, DC 20007

202-342-3200
Announcement. Memorandum to applicants, "Application procedure and related information."

46. *Name:*   *Dumbarton Oaks Center for Byzantine Studies*
Trustees for Harvard University
Type: Summer fellowships
Purpose: Research in Byzantine Civilization in all its aspects, including relations with neighboring cultures. Fields include the late Roman and early Christian period, and the Middle Ages generally. Comparative studies of Byzantine culture exchanges with the Latin West and with Slavic and Near Eastern countries are encouraged. Fellowships are offered in art history, archaeology, architecture, history, law, music, philology, philosophy, theology, and other disciplines.
Support: Housing accomodations, plus a limited number of stipends, the size of which will be determined by need and the length of time to be spent at Dumbarton Oaks.
Duration: Varies, depending on the project. Requests for between 4 and 8 weeks will be given priority.
Deadline: To be announced each Fall.
Inquiries: The Assistant Director
Dumbarton Oaks
1703 32nd St., N.W.
Washington, DC 20007
202-342-3200
Announcement. Memorandum to fellowship applicants, "Application procedures and related information."

47. *Name:*   *Harry and Jane Fischel Foundation*
Type: Grants
Purpose: To develop Talmudic research.
Inquiries: Harry and Jane Fischel Foundation
276 Fifth Ave.
New York, NY 10001
212-684-2626

48. *Name:*   *Folger Shakespeare Library*
Type: Fellowships
Purpose: Research at the Library in Renaissance and 18th century studies (literature, history, philosophy, music, art, and others) and in history of drama.
Support: Because of major renovation and expansion of the Library, all activities, including fellowship program, have been temporarily suspended. It is estimated that applications for fellowships will not be acted upon until Summer 1980.

Inquiries: O. B. Hardison, Director
Folger Shakespeare Library
201 E. Capital St.
Washington, DC 20003
202-546-4800

49. *Name:* *Gennadius Library* (American School of Classical Studies at Athens)
Type: Fellowship in Post-Classical Greek Studies
Purpose: To encourage younger scholars to establish themselves in later Greek studies.
Support: $3,500.
Deadline: 20 January for application and supporting letters. Announcement by 1 April.
Inquiries: J.A.S. Evans
Chairman of the Gennadius Library Committee
Department of Classics, University of British Columbia
Vancouver, British Columbia V6T 1W5
Canada
604-228-2889
Inquiries and application forms.

50. *Name:* *German Academic Exchange Service* (DAAD)
Type: Information visits by groups of professors and students
Purpose: "To increase the knowledge of specific German subjects and/or institutions within the framework of an academic study tour."
Number: Varies.
Support: Program arrangement, financial assistance on per person/per diem basis.
Conditions: Tours are for a minimum of 7 days, a maximum of 21 days. No tours are organized for July and August.
Deadline: 31 July; 16 October; 15 December; 31 March.
N.B. Applications must be received at least six months prior to departure date.
Inquiries: German Academic Exchange Service
535 Fifth Ave., Suite 1107
New York, NY 10017
212-599-0464
Announcement and application form. Specify Ref. no. 7.35.

51. *Name:* *German Academic Exchange Services* (DAAD)
Type: Short term research fellowships
Purpose: To allow advanced graduate students or those recently awarded the doctorate to pursue independent research.
Number: Varies.
Support: Monthly maintenance allowance. Fellow must provide own travel.

Conditions:	Applicant must be *ABD* or have a recent *Ph.D.* 18–32 years old. Good knowledge of German required.
Duration:	2 to 6 months during calendar year.
Deadline:	31 October; 31 January; 31 March.
Inquiries:	German Academic Exchange Service 535 Fifth Ave., Suite 1107 New York, NY 10017 212-599-0464 Announcement and application forms. Specify Ref. no. 7.26. *or* Deutscher Akademischer Austauschdienst Kennedyallee 50 D-53 Bonn-Bad Godesberg Federal Republic of Germany

52. *Name:* German *Academic Exchange Service* (Deutsche Akademischer Austauschdienst)

Type:	Study and research grants
Purpose:	Study or research at a university or research institute in Germany.
Number:	About 50 annually.
Support:	Maintenance, international travel expenses, plus allowance for spouse. Travel expenses, health insurances, book grant, adjustment allowance, tuition waver.
Conditions:	Candidates on *graduate, doctoral,* and *postdoctoral* level. 18 to 32 years. Working knowledge of German.
Duration:	7 to 10 months during academic year.
Deadline:	Applications 12–16 months ahead of time. Deadline 1 November at the Institute of International Education, earlier at universities.
Inquiries:	Campus Fulbright advisor (for students) *or* German Academic Exchange Service 535 Fifth Ave., Suite 1107 New York, NY 10017 212-599-0464 Announcement and application forms. *or* Institute of International Education (for at-large applicants) 809 United Nations Plaza New York, NY 10017 212-883-8200

53. *Name:* German *Academic Exchange Service* (DAAD)

Type:	Study visits
Purpose:	To allow teachers and researchers with the *Ph.D* to pur-

sue independent research in the Federal Republic of Germany.

Number: Varies.

Support: Monthly maintenance allowance. Travel within Germany (but no international travel).

Conditions: At least 2 years' teaching and/or research experience after the Ph.D.

Duration: Up to 3 months during calendar year.

Deadlines: 31 October; 31 January; 31 March.

Inquiries: German Academic Exchange Service
535 Fifth Ave., Suite 1107
New York, NY 10017
212-599-0464
Announcement and application forms. Specify Ref. no. 7.23.

54. *Name:* *German Marshall Fund of the United States*

Type: Fellowships

Purpose: To support projects that "contribute to a better understanding of significant contemporary problems common to industrial societies."

Number: About 12 annually.

Support: A stipend equal to Fellow's current income (within a fixed maximum). One transatlantic round-trip economy fare for Fellow. Similar travel expenses to a Fellow's accompanying spouse and minor children if for a period exceeding four months. Fellowship does not support research assistance, computer time, housing, insurance, benefits, and other direct or indirect project costs.

Conditions: *Established scholars* with *advanced degrees* in any field. Fellowship is for full-time research. The following issues are of current priority interest to the Fund: urban and metropolitan development, administration, finance, and services; employment and labor market policies; labor relations; working conditions; women's employment and other labor force changes (youth, migrants, etc.); policies affecting families; environmental and growth management policies; administration of criminal and juvenile justice; comparative social policies; and issues of international interdependence, excluding military, security, or defense affairs. While the Fund gives preference to these topics, it may consider research focused on other issues common to industrial societies. The Fund also supports projects resulting in new interdisciplinary perspectives and in the development of working relations between U.S. and European scholars. Each project must have U.S. and European (Western and/or Eastern) components, but may also involve other countries. Sabbatical and other grants may be held during tenure of the Fellowship.

Duration: 1 academic term or longer.
Deadline: 30 November.
Inquiries: The German Marshall Fund of the United States
11 Dupont Circle, N.W.
Washington, DC 20036
202-797-6430
Announcement and application forms.

55. *Name:* *Graham Foundation for Advanced Studies in the Fine Arts*
Type Grants
Purpose: Advanced study in architecture and the fine arts contributive to it.
Number: Varies: aproximately 50 annually.
Support: Up to about $10,000.
Conditions: Grants principally to *Americans* working within the U.S. Must have outstanding talent, specific work objectives.
Inquiries: Graham Foundation for Advanced Studies in the Fine Arts
4 W. Burton Place
Chicago, IL 60610
312-787-4071

56. *Name:* *John Simon Guggenheim Memorial Foundation*
Type: Fellowships
Purpose: Research in any field or artistic creation in any fine art.
Number: About 330 annually (300 to U.S. and Canadian citizens; 30 to citizens of the rest of the Western hemisphere and the Philippines).
Support: Varies according to the needs of each Fellow (1978 average $15,600). Foundation may also subsidize publication of Fellowship holder's work.
Conditions: *Candidates* usually 30–45 years old. Demonstrated capacity for productive scholarship (indicated by publication) or unusual creative ability in the fine arts (but not in the performing arts).
Duration: 1 year (appointments for periods as short as 6 months will be considered). May not be renewed immediately.
Deadline: 1 October (for U.S. and Canadian Fellowships).
15 October (for U.S. Fellows seeking further assistance).
1 December (for western hemisphere and Philippines fellowships).
15 December (for western hemisphere and Philippine Fellows seeking further assistance).
Inquiries: John Simon Guggenheim Memorial Foundation
90 Park Ave.

New York, NY 10016
212-687-4470
Brochure.

57. *Name*
    Type:
    Purpose:

    Number:
    Support:
    Conditions:

George and Eliza Gardiner Howard Foundation Fellowship
Fellowship
For research in the arts, social sciences, and humanities. To aid the scholarly development of individuals at the mid-point of their careers.
About 5 annually.
Up to $7,000 per year, not renewable.
Candidates must normally be 30 to 40 years old. Fellowship may not be used for degree study. Fellowships are granted on a rotational basis in the following areas:
for 1980–81
  a) Fine, applied, and performing arts (including music, theater, film, art history, musicology, and media-related projects, playwriting).
for 1981–82
  b) Literature and languages (including criticism, linguistics, foreign language studies, creative writing exclusive of playwriting).
for 1982–83
  c) Social sciences, history, philosophy, and science related projects (including anthropology, archaeology, religion).
Candidates must be nominated: those with academic affiliations by their institutions (which may nominate only 2 annually); those without institutional affiliations by an institution (e.g., museum) or appropriate professional (critic, editor of academic journal, etc.).

Duration: 1 year, beginning 1 July.
Deadline: 1 November for nominations.
1 December for completed applications.
Announcements 15 April.
Inquiries: Graduate School
Brown University
Box 1867
Providence, RI 02912
401-863-2600

58. *Name:*
    Type:
    Purpose:

Alexander von Humboldt Foundation
Postdoctoral research fellowships
To provide opportunities for young, highly qualified scholars from around the world to carry out specific research projects of their own choice in the Federal Republic of Germany and in West Berlin; projects are

	carried out at a university or research institute.
Number:	About 450 per year.
Support:	Research fellowship pays between DM 1900 and DM 2600 monthly, according to qualifications, plus family and travel allowance. Grants for two to four month German language course in Germany prior to the beginning of the Fellowship are available.
Duration:	6 to 12 months in Germany. Extensions of up to 2 years possible.
Conditions:	Fellowships are for specific research projects, not for training purposes, short term study tours, or participation in conferences. Candidates must either have a *doctorate* or have attained comparable academic qualifications through research, teaching, and academic publications. Applicants must have adequate command of German and must not have exceeded 40 years of age.
Deadline:	Applications may be submitted at any time. The selection committee meets three times yearly, in March, July, and November. A *complete* application should be submitted 4 months before the committee's meeting.
Inquiries:	German Academic Exchange Service

535 Fifth Ave., Suite 1107
New York, NY 10017
212-599-0464
or
The embassy or consulates of the Federal Republic of Germany.
or
Alexander von Humboldt—Stiftung
Jean-Paul-Strasse 12
D-5300 Bonn 2
Federal Republic of Germany
Tele: (0-22-21) 36-3021
Announcement and application form.

59. *Name:*	*Hungarian Cultural Foundation*
Type:	Fellowships and grants
Purpose:	Study and research in any aspect of Hungarian culture.
Support:	Varies, averages $1000. Renewal possible.
Conditions:	Some matching funds required.
Deadline:	Any time.
Inquiries:	Professor Joseph M. Ertavy-Barath

Hungarian Cultural Foundation
Box 364
Stone Mountain, GA 30083

60. *Name:*	*Henry E. Huntington Library and Art Gallery*
Type:	a. Research awards

b. Huntington Library—NEH Fellowships

For research using the materials of the Huntington Library in English or American literature or history.

Number: About 40 research awards annually; 3 or 4 NEH fellowships.

Support: a. $600 per month for awards with period of less than six months (purpose of these is to supplement reduced pay of scholars on leave or sabbatical).
b. For NEH fellowship, stipends are adjusted to need. They are ordinarily set at one-half cash salary of applicant, but may not exceed $1667 per month.

Conditions: Candidates must have *advanced degree.* Research must be undertaken at the Library. Program favors scholars with a good publishing record. Awards for projects that complement one another (but not for projects that duplicate one another) may be held simultaneously. NEH fellowships may not be awarded to foreign nationals unless they have been U.S. residents for at least three years.

Duration: a. From 1 month to 6 months for research awards.
b. From 6 to 12 months for NEH fellowship.

Deadline: Between 1 October and 31 December for awards within the twelve month period beginning on the following 1 June.

Inquiries: The Director
Huntington Library and Art Gallery
San Marino, CA 91108
213-792-6141
Brochure: "Research Awards at the Huntington Library."

61. *Name:* *IFK-International Courses in German Language and Philology* (Salzburg)

Type: Scholarships for summer courses

Purpose: Courses in German language and philology, in association with the University of Salzburg and the Goethe Institute (Munich).

Number: 10 each summer.

Support: 5000 Austrian schillings.

Conditions: No restriction as to nationality. *Applicants* should attach curriculum vitae and references to their application letters.

Duration: 3–4 weeks.

Deadline: 31 March (early Fall, through Institute of International Education).

Inquiries: International Courses in German Language and Philology
IFK-Franz-Josef-Strasse 19

A-5020 Salzburg, Austria
or
Institute of International Education
809 United Nations Plaza
New York, NY 10017
212-883-8477

62. *Name:*   *Immigration History Research Center* (University of Minnesota)

    Type: Grants-in-aid to students of American immigration and ethnic history

    Purpose: To aid scholars whose research requires the use of the collections of the Immigration History Research Center.

    Support: Up to $3,000 for travel, living, and research expenses.

    Conditions: Applicants must be qualified *scholars* (doctoral candidate, recent Ph.D.s, and established scholars) studying American immigration and ethnic history. The collections of the Center concentrate on American ethnic groups whose origins are in eastern, central, and southern Europe and in the Middle East. Although the Center's collections are primarily historical in nature, they lend themselves to a variety of disciplinary uses.

    Deadline: Not yet established, contact the Center.

    Inquiries: Immigration History Research Center, Grant-in-Aid Committee
University of Minnesota
826 Berry St.
St. Paul, MN 55114
612-373-5581
Announcement.

63. *Name:*   *Institut Francais de Washington*

    Type: Gilbert Chinard Scholarships

    Purpose: For maintenance during research in France.

    Number: 2 or more, depending on budget and quality of applications.

    Support: $500.

    Conditions: Candidates are either *ABD* or have had the *Ph.D.* for no more than six years before application deadline. Awards are not for travel. Applicants write up to two pages describing research project and details of planned trip to France, and giving curriculum vitae. For Ph.D. candidates, a letter from dissertation advisor. Upon return, a brief report is to be sent to the Institute.

    Duration: At least 2 months.

    Deadline: 1 January.

    Inquiries: Edouard Morot-Sir, President

Institut Francais de Washington
141 Dey Hall, Department of Romance Languages
University of North Carolina at Chapel Hill
Chapel Hill, NC 27514
Announcement.
N.B. Institute also sponsors annual Chinard awards of
$1,000 for the best manuscript(s) in the history of
Franco-American Relations. Inquire at the above
address.

64. *Name:*   *Institute for Advanced Studies in the Humanities*
(University of Edinburgh)

Type: Fellowships

Purpose: Postdoctoral research in the humanities.

Support: Living allowance plus research expenses up to about
£1000; tenable at the Institute. Some fellowships are
without stipend.

Conditions: Candidates must have *doctoral degree* or equivalent qualification and be engaged in advanced research in the
humanities (archaeology, classics, fine arts and musicology, history, language, literature, philosophy, and Scot-
tish studies). Institute accepts applications "from scholars
of established reputation as well as from younger scholars holding a doctorate or offering equivalent evidence
of aptitude for further study."

Duration: 1 term to 1 year.

Deadline: 31 January.

Inquiries: Director of the Institute
Institute for Advanced Studies in the Humanities
University of Edinburgh
17 Buccleuch Place
Edinburgh EH8 9LW, Scotland
Tele: 031-667-1011, ext. 6349
Application forms.

65. *Name:*   *Institute for Advanced Study: School of Historical
Studies*

Type: Appointments

Purpose: Humanities research

Number: 35.

Support: Living expenses at the Institute. Variable stipend for
spring and fall appointments.

Conditions: Most appointments are by invitation, but some members
are selected through letters of application stating a
candidate's research and reasons for admission to the
Institute.

Duration: Fall and/or spring semester.

Deadline: 15 October for fall or spring appointments.

Inquiries: Dr. Harry Woolf, Director
                  Institute for Advanced Study
                  Princeton, NJ 08540
                  609-924-4400

66. *Name:*   *Institute for Research in the Humanities*
                  (University of Wisconsin)
    Type: Fellowships
    Purpose: Post-doctoral research in the humanities (history, philos-
                  ophy, language and literature, humanistic aspects of
                  environmental studies).
    Number: 2 annually.
    Support: $15,000; tenable at the Institute.
    Conditions: Candidates must have *recent doctoral degrees.* Program
                  favors young scholars with well-advanced research
                  projects. Priority is given those whose projects are re-
                  lated to the research of the senior members of the
                  Institute.
    Duration: 1 academic year. Fellowship is held in residence at the
                  Institute.
    Deadline: 15 October.
    Inquiries: Robert N. Kingdon, Director
                  Institute for Research in the Humanities
                  Old Observatory, University of Wisconsin
                  Madison, WI 53706
                  608-262-3855
                  Announcement and application forms.

67. *Name:*   *International Research and Exchanges Board* (IREX)
    Type: Eastern Europe Program for research and study at insti-
                  tutions of higher learning in Bulgaria, Czechoslovakia,
                  Hungary, Poland, Romania, Yugoslavia, and the Ger-
                  man Democratic Republic.
    Number: Quotes vary: 20 to 64 man-months of participation, de-
                  pending on the country.
    Support: Transportation (½ for dependents). Instruction, re-
                  search expenses, language training (except in GDR and
                  Yugoslavia), housing, medical and dental care, local cur-
                  rency allowance (depending on one's circumstances).
                  GDR and Yugoslavia limit housing allowance and dental-
                  medical care to applicant, all others extend these to
                  applicant and dependents.
    Conditions: *U.S. citizens; senior scholars, young faculty* and *ad-
                  vanced graduate students* (*ABD*). Must have a full-time
                  affiliation with a North American college or university,
                  and have the language facility necessary to the research
                  study project.
    Duration: 1 semester or 1 academic year.

Deadline: 1 November.
Inquiries: IREX
655 Third Ave.
New York, NY 10017
212-490-2002
Program announcement.

68. *Name:* *International Research and Exchanges Board* (IREX)
    Type: Exchange of Senior Scholars in all Fields
    Purpose: For research in the Soviet Union under the IREX exchange programs with the Soviet Ministry of Higher and Specialized Secondary Education.
    Number: At least 10 annually.
    Support: Travel, housing, instruction and research costs, medical and dental care for participant, monthly ruble allowance.
    Conditions: *U.S. citizens; senior faculty status* (associate or full professor, but assistant professor may apply). Must have a full-time affiliation with a North American college or university, have a sufficient mastery of Russian for research.
    Duration: 3 to 6 months (not during summer months) at universities and other institutions under the Ministry.
    Deadline: 1 November.
    Inquiries: IREX
655 Third Ave.
New York, NY 10017
212-490-2002
Program announcement.
N.B. 1980 Olympics may disrupt summer programs in major Russian cities.

69. *Name:* *International Research and Exchanges Board* (IREX)
    Type: Exchange of graduate students and young faculty in all fields
    Purpose: For research at Soviet universities under the IREX exchange programs with the Soviet Ministry of Higher and Specialized Secondary Education.
    Number: About 40 annually.
    Support: Travel, housing, instruction and research costs, ruble allowance, medical and dental care for participant and dependents, preliminary language training.
    Conditions: *Graduate students and young faculty; U.S. citizens.* Must have a full-time affiliation with a North American college or university, a sufficient mastery of Russian for research purposes (preliminary language program begins in USSR in August).
    Duration: 1 semester (6 months) to a full academic year (10 months).

Deadline: 1 November.
Inquiries: IREX
                655 Third Ave.
                New York, NY 10017
                212-490-2002
                Program announcement.
                N.B. 1980 Olympics may disrupt summer programs in
                major Russian cities.

70. *Name:*   *International Research and Exchanges Board* (IREX)
    Type: Grants for Collaborative Activities and New Exchanges
    Purpose: "To encourage the development of individual and institu-
                 tional collaboration and exchange involving humanists
                 and social scientists from the United States and from
                 one or more of the exchange countries (U.S.S.R. and
                 Eastern Europe), as well as Albania and Mongolia . . ."
    Support: Less than $10,000.
    Conditions: Eligible for support are "bilateral and multi-national
                 symposia, collaborative and parallel research, joint pub-
                 lications, exchanges of data, comparative surveys and the
                 like, as well as brief visits in the planning of such proj-
                 ects." Proposals must evidence exceptional merit, feasi-
                 bility, and substantial prior planning and consultation.
                 Grants will not support individual study, research, or
                 attendance at scheduled scholarly meetings. IREX will
                 consider preliminary support of university-related ex-
                 changes of students and faculty, but requires university
                 sponsorship of resulting exchanges.
    Duration: Up to 1 year.
    Deadline: 31 March; 31 May; 30 September; 31 December.
                 Decisions announced in one month. Preliminary letters
                 are invited.
    Inquiries: IREX
                 655 Third Ave.
                 New York, NY 10017
                 212-490-2002
                 Program announcement.
                 N.B. 1980 Olympics may disrupt summer programs in
                 major Russian cities.

71. *Name:*   *International Research and Exchanges Board* (IREX)
    Type: Slavonic Studies Seminar in Bulgaria
    Purpose: To improve knowledge of Bulgarian at the Slavonic
                 Studies Seminar at Kliment Okhridski University in Sofia.
    Number: Up to 10 annually.
    Support: Round-trip transportation, lodgings, tuition, and local
                 costs.

Conditions: U.S. citizens; scholars who have a full-time affiliation with a North American college or university (both graduate students and faculty).
Duration: Month of August.
Deadline: 10 January.
Inquiries: IREX
655 Third Ave.
New York, NY 10017
212-490-2002
Program announcement.

72. *Name:* *International Research and Exchanges Board* (IREX)
Type: Soviet Academy of Sciences Exchange of Senior Scholars in the Humanities and Social Sciences
Purpose: For research in the Soviet Union by senior scholars (the program is funded by the American Council of Learned Societies, but administered by IREX).
Number: Varies: 100 months of research support are offered each year; 60 of these months are reserved for individual research visits of between 2 and 10 months, and 40 months are allocated for joint projects under the Commission in Social Science and Humanities.
Support: Research expenses, housing, medical care, per diem ruble allowance. Dependents accompany participant at own expense.
Conditions: U.S. citizens; senior scholar status (professors, associate professors, and in exceptional cases, assistant professors) and distinction in a discipline of the social sciences or humanities. Must have a full-time affiliation with a North American college or university.
Duration: 2 to 10 months (but not in summer).
Deadline: 1 November.
Inquiries: IREX
655 Third Ave.
New York, NY 10017
212-490-2002
Program announcement.
N.B. 1980 Olympics may disrupt summer programs in major Russian cities.

73. *Name:* *International Research and Exchange Board* (IREX)
Type: Summer exchange of language teachers with the USSR
Purpose: Grants for a summer program of language study and methodology at Moscow State University.
Number: At least 35 annually.
Support: Instruction, housing, ruble allowance, and a study-related tour, round-trip travel from home institution to Moscow.
Conditions: U.S. citizens who are teachers of Russian at the college

or secondary school level. Minimum of two years' teaching experience (teaching assistants will be considered). Must have studied Russian in college for four years or the equivalent.

Duration:	About 8 weeks, from mid-June to mid-August.
Deadline:	10 January.
Inquiries:	IREX
	655 Third Ave.
	New York, NY 10017
	212-490-2002
	Program announcement.
	N.B. 1980 Olympics may disrupt summer programs in major Russian cities.

74. *Name:*   *International Research and Exchanges Board* (IREX)
   Type: Travel Grants for Senior Scholars
   Purpose: "To facilitate communication between prominent American humanists and social scientists and their colleagues in the countries with which IREX conducts exchanges (the U.S.S.R. and Eastern Europe), as well as in Albania and Mongolia."
   Support: Round-trip economy transportation.
   Conditions: Applicants must have received a formal invitation from an appropriate institution in one of these countries (such as an academy of sciences or one of its institutions) for the purpose of consultation, lecturing, or the like. Preference normally given to scholars outside the fields of Soviet or East European studies. Grants are not for individual study or research, or for attendance at scheduled meetings. Recipients must make their own visa and travel arrangements.
   Duration: Less than 2 months.
   Deadline: 31 March; 31 May; 30 September; 31 December.
   Inquiries: IREX
  655 Third Ave.
  New York, NY 10017
  212-490-2002
  Program announcement.
  N.B. 1980 Olympics may disrupt summer programs in major Russian cities.

75. *Name:*   *Japan Foundation*
   Type: Education Abroad Program
   Purpose: Language training in Japan or first hand study of Japanese culture and society for groups of students and teachers.
   Number: 2 or 3 annually.
   Support: Partial payments for group's transportation, living ex-

penses, tuition, and related fees (made on a cost-sharing basis). Foundation's contribution will not exceed $10,000.

Conditions: Applicants should "provide details indicating advance preparation for the proposed trip." Visits should be part of an on-going program "which has the potential to engage students or teachers in a more durable interest in Japanese studies."

Duration: A "significant" duration (i.e., more than 2 weeks).

Deadline: 1 December.

Inquiries: The Japan Foundation
Watergate Office Bldg., Suite 570
600 New Hampshire Ave., N.W.
Washington, DC 20037
202-965-4313
Brochures and application forms.

76. *Name:*   *Japan Foundation*

    Type: Professional Fellowships (short and long term)

    Purpose: "To assist scholars and other professionals in the United States who are engaged in a study relating to Japanese culture and society by offering an opportunity to conduct their research in Japan."

    Number: 15 long-term; 5 short-term.

    Support: *Long-term:* 300,000 yen monthly (about $1346) for seminar specialists and faculty members. 240,000 yen monthly (about $1091) for specialists and faculty members at an early state of their careers. Monthly housing allowance, limited monthly dependent allowance, settling-in allowance, luggage allowance, research-travel allowance, and document allowance. Tuition and fees when necessary. Economy round-trip air travel to Tokyo for Fellow only.

      Short-term: economy round-trip air travel to Tokyo for Fellow only. Monthly housing allowance and research-travel allowance.

    Conditions: *U.S. citizens* or permanent residents. Fellows must devote full time to their projects; no other fellowships or major grants may be held concurrently. Applicants are:

      a. Faculty members, writers, artists, or other professionals with substantial training or experience in Japanese studies.

      b. Faculty members whose specialization is not Japanese studies but who wish to increase their professional competence in the Japanese field.

      c. Translators from Japanese into English, librarians concerned with Japanese studies, or museum staff members who deal with Japanese works of art.

Fellowships are tenable only in Japan. Grantees may apply for other fellowships only after three years beyond the completion of their fellowships.

Duration: 4 to 12 months for long term.
2 to 3 months (in the summer) for short term.
(Extensions are normally not considered.)
Each program conforms to the Japanese fiscal year of 1 April to 31 March.

Deadline: 1 December (announcements in late March).

Inquiries: The Japan Foundation
Watergate Office Bldg., Suite 570
600 New Hampshire Ave., N.W.
Washington, DC 20037
202-965-4313
Brochures and application forms.

77. *Name:* *Kevorkian Foundation*
Type: Grants
Purpose: Study and research in Near and Middle Eastern art.
Inquiries: Kevorkian Foundation
1411 Third Ave.
New York, NY 10028
212-988-9304

78. *Name:* *Kate Neal Kinley Memorial Fellowship*
Type: Fellowship
Purpose: Advanced study of architecture (design or history), art, or music.
Support: $3500 for one academic year; tenable anywhere.
Conditions: Candidates must be *graduates* of superior institutions of the fine arts or graduates whose major studies have been in architecture, art, or music.
Deadline: 15 April.
Inquiries: Kate Neal Kinley Memorial Fellowship
College of Fine and Applied Arts, 110 Architecture Bldg.
University of Illinois
Urbana, IL 61801
217-333-1000

79. *Name:* *Kosciuszko Foundation*
Type: Grants
Purpose: For research and study at institutions of higher learning in Poland.
Support: Partial transportation, medical, 2400 zl per month living allowance, housing, tuition. Higher benefits for faculty.
Conditions: *U.S. or Canadian citizens; university faculty* and *graduate students (ABD).*
Duration: 1 academic year (renewable).

Deadline:	15 January.
Inquiries:	The Kosciuszko Foundation
	15 E. 65th St.
	New York, NY 10021
	Attn: Exchange Programs
	212-734-2130, -2131
	N.B. These programs are being revised for 1980. Send for brochure.

80. *Name:*   *Kosciuszko Foundation*

Type:	Scholarship and research grants
Purpose:	Tuition scholarship for graduate students of Polish background, in any field of study. Research grants for persons of any ethnic background pursuing studies in Polish history or culture.
Support:	Generally $1000 yearly.
Conditions:	Some grants restricted to American citizens and/or to persons of Polish descent or birth.
Duration:	1 academic year (renewable).
Deadline:	15 January.
Inquiries:	The Kosciuszko Foundation
	15 E. 65th St.
	New York, NY 10021
	Attn: Scholarship Programs
	212-734-2130, -2131
	N.B. These programs are being revised for 1980. Send for brochure.

81. *Name:*   *Kosciuszko Foundation*

Type:	Summer study programs in Poland
Purpose:	Courses in Polish language, history, and culture at various Polish universities. Specialized courses in the arts and other fields.
Support:	Major costs paid by participants, some aid available.
Conditions:	High school graduation minimum requirement. Most courses require no previous knowledge of Polish.
Duration:	4 to 6 weeks.
Deadline:	31 January.
Inquiries:	Kosciuszko Foundation
	15 E. 65th St.
	New York, NY 10021
	Attn: Summer Sessions
	212-734-2130, -2131
	N.B. These programs are being revised for 1980. Send for brochure.

82. *Name:*   *Samuel H. Kress Foundation*

Type:	Grants

Purpose:	Subvents scholarly publication, especially in art history and connoisseurship. Supports restoration projects.
Inquiries:	Samuel H. Kress Foundation 221 W. 57th St. New York, NY 10019 212-586-4450

83. *Name:*   *George C. Marshall Memorial Fund in Denmark*

Type:	Fellowships
Purpose:	To support a professional study program, an academic study program, or a research project in Denmark.
Number:	15–20 awards for 1979–80.
Support:	D.kr. 32,000 (app. $5000) for twelve months for all expenses. Grants for programs of shorter duration will be correspondingly lower.
Conditions:	*American citizen;* B.A. degree. Well-defined program of study or research. Age 40 maximum (program favors younger candidates who have not previously studied in Denmark). Danish language facility as required by project.
Duration:	3 to 12 months, renewable.
Deadline:	1 November.
Inquiries:	Exchange Division American-Scandanavian Foundation 127 E. 73 St. New York, NY 10021 212-879-9779 Announcement.

84. *Name:*   *Andrew W. Mellon Faculty Fellowships in the Humanities* (Harvard University)

Type:	Fellowships for nontenured young scholars and teachers in the humanities
Purpose:	"To offer promising humanists an opportunity to demonstrate their scholarly potential at a critical point in their careers . . . to enable them to broaden their intellectual range and to develop their teaching skills."
Number:	Approximately 15 annually.
Support:	Salary of $16,000. Full access to libraries. "Benefits of membership in the Harvard University community."
Conditions:	*Earned Ph.D.* Two years' postdoctoral teaching in the humanities at the college or university level (usually as an assistant professor), nontenured. Fellows will hold one-year appointments with departmental affiliation. Each Fellow is required to teach in the Freshman Seminar Program or a departmental course.
Duration:	1 year. Appointments begin 1 July, but residence is not expected until 1 September.

Deadline:	1 November. Awards announced 30 January.
Inquiries:	Dr. Richard M. Hunt, Program Director
	Harvard University Mellon Faculty Fellowships
	Lamont Library 202
	Cambridge, MA 02138
	617-495-2519
	Announcement describes application procedure.

85. *Name:*   *Andrew W. Mellon Postdoctoral Fellowships in the Humanities* (Stanford University)

Type: Fellowships for highly promising young scholar teachers in the humanities

Purpose: To offer young scholars and teachers the opportunity for scholarly work and intellectual growth.

Support: Annual stipend of $14,500.

Conditions: Ph.D. earned after June 1975 (five years before commencement of fellowship) and before September 1980 (date of commencement of fellowship). Fellowship offers a nonfaculty one-year position with departmental affiliation and limited teaching duties. Applications will be accepted in the following disciplines: art history, classics, drama history, English, history, history of science, linguistics, music history, philosophy, religious studies, comparative literature, and languages and literature (Asian, Slavic, French, German, Italian, Portuguese, Spanish).

Duration: 1 year (renewable).

Deadline: 1 December (but application should be sent as early as possible).

Inquiries: Mellon Application
c/o The Dean
School of Humanities and Sciences
Stanford University
Stanford, CA 94305
415-497-2300
Announcement and application form.

86. *Name:*   *Andrew Mellon Postdoctoral Fellowships* (University of Pittsburgh)

Type: Post-doctoral fellowships

Purpose: Advanced study and research in the humanities (classics, English, history and philosophy of science, fine arts, music, musicology, philosophy and modern languages), social sciences (including anthropology and history), and natural sciences. "To foster the professional development of young scholars who give promise of achieving distinction in their fields."

Number: Approximately 7 annually.

Support: $12,000 for eleven months, plus a small supplement for travel expenses (up to $200) and research costs; or $9,800 for nine months, plus a small travel and research supplement.

Conditions: Candidates must be *young scholars* who give promise of achieving in their fields. They are expected to remain in Pittsburgh for research and writing during the tenure of the fellowship.

Duration: 9 or 11 months' residence in Pittsburgh. Academic year begins 1 September.

Deadline: 15 January.

Inquiries: Andrew Mellon Postdoctoral Fellowships
Director of Graduate Programs, FAS
1028-H Cathedral of Learning
University of Pittsburgh
Pittsburgh, PA 15260
412-624-4141
Announcement and application form.

87. *Name:*   *Memorial Foundation for Jewish Culture*
    Type: Grants
    Purpose: To support independent research in any field of Jewish studies.
    Support: Up to $1500.
    Conditions: *Applicants* must be recognized or qualified scholars, researchers, or artists.
    Deadline: 30 November.
    Inquiries: Dr. Jerry Hochbaum, Associate Executive Director
Memorial Foundation for Jewish Culture
15 E. 26th St.
New York, NY 10010
212-679-4074

88. *Name:*   *Metropolitan Museum of Art* (New York)
    Type: Chester Dale Fellowship
    Purpose: Research in history of western art. Fellowships provide for independent study or for research related to the collections of the Museum and carried out at the Museum.
    Number: 4 annually.
    Support: Varies; $3,000–$10,000 per year. Possibility for renewal.
    Conditions: Painters, sculptors, art historians, and art critics whose fields are related to the fine arts of the western world and who are preferably *American citizens* under forty.
    Duration: 3 months to 1 year.
    Deadline: 11 January. Announcements by 3 March.
    Inquiries: Secretary of the Grants Committee
Metropolitan Museum of Art
Fifth Ave. & 82nd St.

New York, NY 10028
212-879-5500
Announcement.

89. Name: *Metropolitan Museum of Art* (New York)
    Type: Andrew W. Mellon Fellowships
    Purpose: "For *promising young scholars* with commendable research projects related to the Museum's collections, as well as for *distinguished visiting scholars* from this country and abroad, who can serve as teachers and advisors and make their expertise available to catalogue and refine the collections."
    Number: 8.
    Support: $7500 ($15,000 for distinguished visitors), plus $1000 for travel and research expenses.
    Conditions: Applicants should have received the *doctorate* or have completed substantial work toward it. Term of fellowship should be spent at the Museum.
    Duration: Maximum of 1 year.
    Deadline: 11 January. Announcements by 3 March.
    Inquiries: Secretary of the Grants Committee
                Metropolitan Museum of Art
                Fifth Ave. & 82nd St.
                New York, NY 10028
                212-879-5500
                Announcement.

90. Name: *Metropolitan Museum of Art* (New York)
    Type: Andrew W. Mellon Fellowships in the Conservation of Paintings
    Purpose: Fellowships for advanced students of the conservation of paintings to work in the Paintings Conservation Department of the Museum and to study in Europe during the summer months.
    Number: 2.
    Support: $13,500 for the first year; $14,000 for the second year. $2,000 per year for summer travel.
    Conditions: Applicants must be "*American citizens* at an advanced level in their training in the conservation of paintings and with some years of practical experience."
    Duration: 2 years.
    Deadline: 1 February.
    Inquiries: John M. Brealey, Conservator
                Metropolitan Museum of Art
                Fifth Ave. & 82nd St.
                New York, NY 10028
                212-879-5500
                Announcement.

91. *Name:*   *Metropolitan Museum of Art* (New York)
    Type: J. Clawson Mills Scholarships
    Purpose: Research in art history, for those wishing to carry out a research project related to the collections of the Museum.
    Number: 2 annually.
    Support: $6000 per year.
    Conditions: Tenable at the Museum. Reserved for *mature scholars* of demonstrated ability.
    Duration: 1 year; possibility of renewal.
    Deadline: 11 January. Announcements by 3 March.
    Inquiries: Secretary of the Grants Committee
                  Metropolitan Museum of Art
                  1000 Fifth Ave.
                  New York, NY 10028
                  212-879-5500
                  Announcement.

92. *Name:*   *National Council of Teachers of English Research Foundation*
    Type: Grants in Aid
    Purpose: To support "any organized inquiry, theoretical or applied, into the subject of English, including the language arts of related fields, which has significance for the teaching or learning of English."
    Support: Varies.
    Conditions: Grants are for "qualified individuals or groups for research into the teaching or learning of English at any level of instruction." Travel costs and subsidies for loss of salary may be requested only if applicant's institution or cooperating school bears larger portion of the cost.
    Deadline: 15 February. Announcement in early spring.
    Inquiries: Executive Secretary
                  National Council of Teachers of English
                  1111 Kenyon Rd.
                  Urbana, IL 61801
                  217-328-3870
                  Brochure, instruction, and application forms.

93. *Name:*   *National Endowment for the Humanities* (NEH)
                  Division of Fellowships
    Type: NEH Fellowships
    Number: About 330 annually.
    Support: Categories A and B fellowships: $10,000 (for 6 months) or $20,000 (for 12 months). Category C: $20,000 (for 12 months).
    Conditions: Fellowships are offered in three categories:
                  Category A. These are fellowships for independent study

and research for scholars, teachers, and others whose work seems likely to lead to significant contributions to humanistic thought and knowledge. Applications are encouraged from persons with broad interpretive interests as well as from scholars working in specialized fields. Nonacademic applicants are welcome.

Category B. These are fellowships for independent study and research for persons engaged primarily in undergraduate teaching, whose work will enhance their ability as teachers as well as make an important contribution to humanistic thought and knowledge. Applicants should be primarily engaged in, or intending careers in, undergraduate teaching. They will normally be teaching in undergraduate or master's degree institutions, but faculty members in doctoral institutions who are predominantly engaged in teaching undergraduate courses, particularly scholars in the early years of their careers, are also eligible.

Category C. These fellowships provide opportunities to undergraduate college teachers to participate in seminars directed by distinguished scholars at designated universities and to undertake research and study of their own choosing over and above the work of the seminars. They enable college teachers to work in a library suitable for advanced study and to discuss their work with the seminar director and with other seminar participants from across the country. To be eligible, applicants must have faculty positions in two-year, four-year, or five-year colleges or universities in the United States at the time of their application. Faculty members of departments with doctoral programs are not eligible to apply these fellowships. Preference is given to applicants who have been teaching at the college level for at least three years.

Deadline: Categories A and B: check with NEH; 1 June in 1980 (for fellowships beginning after 1 January 1981).
Category C: 12 November.

Inquiries: Division of Fellowships
Mail Stop 101
National Endowment for the Humanities
806 15th St., N.W.
Washington, DC 20506
202-724-0238 Director and Deputy Director, Division of Fellowships
202-724-0333 Program Officers, Fellowships: Categories A, B, and C
Preliminary inquiries, application forms, and *Program Announcement.*

94. *Name:*   *National Endowment for the Humanities* (NEH)
                 Division of Fellowships
     Type: Summer Seminars for College Teachers
     Number: About 120 annually, each with 12 members.
     Conditions: This program is intended to provide opportunities during the summer for teachers at undergraduate and two-year colleges to work in their areas of interest with distinguished scholars at institutions with library resources suitable for advanced study. The seminars will be held at institutions broadly distributed throughout the country. A few seminars may be located abroad.

                 Summer Seminar Participants. Applicants must have been teaching for at least three years at two-year, four-year, or five-year colleges or universities. Faculty members of departments with doctoral programs in the humanities are normally not eligible to apply. The stipend amount is $2,500 to cover travel expenses to and from the seminar location, books and other research expenses, and living expenses for a tenure period of two full months. A list of the seminars to be offered each summer will be publicized widely the previous December and will also be available from the Division of Fellowships. College teachers desiring application instructions will be asked to write directly to the seminar director offering the seminar they wish to attend.

                 Summer Seminar Directors. Scholars interested in directing Summer Seminars may obtain proposal guidelines from the Fellowships Division.
     Deadline: Check with NEH.
                 Participants: 1 April (for summer of same year).
                 Directors: 1 July (for summer of subsequent year).
     Inquiries: Division of Fellowships
                 Mail Stop 101
                 National Endowment for the Humanities
                 806 15th St., N.W.
                 Washington, DC 20506
                 202-724-0238 Director and Deputy Director, Division of Fellowships
                 202-724-0376 Program Director, Summer Stipends
                 Preliminary inquiries, application forms, and *Program Announcement.*

95. *Name:*   *National Endowment for the Humanities* (NEH)
                 Division of Fellowships
     Type: Summer Stipends
     Number: About 230 annually.
     Conditions: Summer Stipends are intended for college, junior college, and university faculty members, and others working in

the humanities who have made, or who demonstrate promise of making, a significant contribution in their fields. Each Summer Stipend provides $2,500 for two consecutive months of full-time study or research. The purpose of the stipend is to free recipients from paid summer employment and to provide support for travel and other research expenses so that they can devote this period to concentrated study and research. The work proposed may be within the applicants' special areas of interest, or it may be in some field that will enable them to understand their own fields better and enlarge their competence. The proposed project may be one that can be completed during the stipend period or it may be part of a long-range project. These stipends are available to senior as well as to younger scholars. An applicant for a Summer Stipend employed by a college or university must be nominated by the president, dean, or other designated officer of the institution of employment. Every college and university in the United States and its territorial possessions may nominate three members of its faculty or staff for a Summer Stipend, basing selection on their ability or promise as scholars or teachers. Of the three nominees selected by the institution, two should be in an early stage of their careers, and one should be in a more advanced state. If an institution declines nomination of a member of its faculty because his or her appointment is terminating, the faculty member may apply directly to the Endowment without nomination. Persons not employed by colleges or universities may apply directly to the Endowment.

Deadline: 15 October (for stipends for summer of following year).
Inquiries: Divisions of Fellowships
Mail Stop 101
National Endowment for the Humanities
806 15th St., N.W.
Washington, DC 20506
202-724-2038 Director and Deputy Director, Division of Fellowships
202-724-0376 Program Officer, Summer Stipends
Preliminary inquiries, application forms, and *Program Announcement.*

96. *Name:*   *National Endowment for the Humanities* (NEH)
Division of Research Grants
Type: Research Collections Program Grants
Duration: Up to 3 years.
Conditions: The purpose of the Research Collections Program is to make the raw materials of research more accessible to

scholars. The Program helps to develop collections either by microfilming materials in foreign repositories so that they will be available in the United States or by collecting data through oral history techniques. It increases access through projects which address national problems in the archival and library field, pilot projects in systems development and library automation which will serve as models in that field, and processing grants to catalog, inventory, or otherwise gain bibliographic control of significant research collections. It is the third type of project which is supported most often by the Collections Program. This program also provides small grants for consultants to evaluate collections in which no archival experts are in residence but which contain materials important to scholarly research and to advise on preparation of a professional work plan for processing such materials. The third objective of the program, encouragement of the use of important research collections, is achieved by projects for long-term collaborative research focused upon and making intensive use of unique collections of research resources. In all cases, a substantial contribution from the sponsoring institution is required.

Deadline: 1 December (for projects beginning 1 July of following year).

Inquiries: The Division of Research Grants
Mail Stop 350
National Endowment for the Humanities
806 15th St., N.W.
Washington, DC 20506
202-724-0226 Director and Deputy Director, Division of Research Grants
202-724-0341 Assistant Director, Research Collecting
Preliminary inquiries, application forms, and *Program Announcement.*

97. *Name:* *National Endowment for the Humanities* (NEH)
Division of Research Grants
Type: Research Conferences Grants
Conditions: The Division supports conferences, symposia, and workshops designed to communicate and assess current research needs and directions or make plans to improve conditions for research. The program supports basic research in the humanities, seeking thereby to encourage and aid open discussion and public dissemination of ideas of either a general or specific nature necessary to an understanding of one or more of the humanistic disciplines.

Deadline: Applications accepted at any time.
Inquiries: The Division of Research Grants
                Mail Stop 350
                National Endowment for the Humanities
                806 15th St., N.W.
                Washington, DC 20506
                202-724-0226 Director and Deputy Director, Division of
                Research Grants
                Preliminary inquiries, application forms, and *Program
                Announcement.*

98. *Name:*   *National Endowment for the Humanities* (NEH)
                Division of Research Grants
    Type: Research Publications Program Grants
    Conditions: The Division considers for subvention of up to $10,000
                per volume proposals from presses and publishing houses
                interested in publishing the direct products of Endow-
                ment grants. The publishing program is not restricted to
                the Division's own grant-products. Eligible manuscripts
                may have been funded in any Endowment program or
                division. No publishing house will receive more than a
                total of $30,000 in such subvention grants in any one
                year. Works of the highest merit in any humanistic field
                which are not the products of previous Endowment
                awards will also be eligible on a limited basis. No pub-
                lisher may submit more than a single application for
                support of materials of this kind in any one cycle.
    Deadline: 15 May (for projects beginning 1 September of same
                year).
                15 November (for projects peginning after 1 March of
                following year).
    Inquiries: The Division of Research Grants
                Mail Stop 350
                National Endowment for the Humanities
                806 15th St., N.W.
                Washington, DC 20506
                202-724-0226 Director and Deputy Director, Division of
                Research Grants
                Preliminary inquiries, application forms, and *Program
                Announcement.*

99. *Name:*   *National Endowment for the Humanities* (NEH)
                Division of Research Grants, General Research Program
    Type: Basic Research Grants
    Conditions: Research in all fields of the humanities that does not de-
                pend on the use of special editing, bibliographic, or archi-
                val skills can be supported through this program. Projects
                tend to be long or middle-term and involve the efforts of

several scholars and other individuals at the professional, assistant, and clerical levels. Suitable projects encompass research that meets a pressing scholarly need, explores the conceptual foundations of disciplines in the humanities, together with studies of their methodologies, and advances a fresh understanding of matters important to scholarship in the humanities. Consideration can also be given to projects that undertake to present the humanities to a readership beyond the schools. This program provides support for American and foreign archaeology —excavations, materials analysis, curatorial, research and prepublication work. Area studies and cross-disciplinary studies are especially appropriate to this category.

Deadline: 1 March (for projects beginning 1 September of same year).
1 September (for projects beginning after 1 March of following year).

Inquiries: The Division of Research Grants
Mail Stop 350
National Endowment for the Humanities
806 15th St., N.W.
Washington, DC 20506
202-724-0226 Director and Deputy Director, Division of Research Grants
202-724-0276 Assistant Director, General Research
Preliminary inquiries, application forms, and *Program Announcement.*

100. *Name:* *National Endowment for the Humanities* (NEH)
Division of Research Grants, General Research Program
Type: State, Local, and Regional History Grants
Conditions: The program supports research and development of new materials and methods useful both to professional scholars and to members of historical societies and organizations, museums, and others seriously concerned with the study of the nation's heritage. Grants are made to prepare materials, collect resources, and produce and disseminate studies; the theoretical conceptions underlying the research should be evident. Grants are made to support individual and collaborative projects.

Deadline: September (for projects beginning after 1 March of following year).

Inquiries: The Division of Research Grants
National Endowment for the Humanities
Mail Stop 350
806 15th St., N.W.
Washington, DC 20506
202-724-0226 Director and Deputy Director, Division of Research Grants

202-724-0276 Assistant Director, General Research
Preliminary inquiries, application forms, and *Program Announcement.*

101. *Name:*   *National Endowment for the Humanities* (NEH)
Division of Research Grants, Research Materials Program

Type: Editing Grants

Conditions: Through grants from its Editing Program, the Endowment strives to make the works and papers of significant authors or historical figures available to the scholar and general reader in authoritative, newly annotated texts. Projects may take the form of editing a single volume, or the collected writings and perhaps hitherto unpublished materials of a figure of major importance to the humanities, or documents from a variety of sources organized to illuminate an historical event or thematic perspective.

Deadline: 1 October (for projects beginning 15 June of following year).

Inquiries: The Division of Research Grants
National Endowment for the Humanities
Mail Stop 350
806 15th St., N.W.
Washington, DC 20506
202-724-0226 Director and Deputy Director, Division of Research Grants
Preliminary inquiries, application forms, and *Program Announcement.*

102. *Name:*   *National Endowment for the Humanities* (NEH)
Division of Research Grants, Research Materials Program

Type: Research Tools Grants

Conditions: This program is designed to support the preparation of reference works considered essential for scholarly research in the humanities and for the more comprehensive dissemination of knowledge throughout the country. To this end, grants from the Research Tools Program have been made to create atlases, bibliographies, dictionaries, encyclopedias, linguistic grammars, concordances, catalogs, and guides.

Deadline: 1 October (for projects beginning 15 June of following year).

Inquiries: The Division of Research Grants
National Endowment for the Humanities
Mail Stop 350
806 15th St., N.W.
Washington, DC 20506
202-724-0226 Director and Deputy Director, Division of

Research Grants
202-724-1672 Assistant Director, Research Tools
Preliminary inquiries, application forms, and *Program Announcement.*

103. *Name:*   *National Endowment for the Humanities* (NEH)
Division of Research Grants, Research Materials Program
Type: Translation Grants
Conditions: This program supports annotated, scholarly translations of works that contribute to an understanding of the history and intellectual achievements of other cultures and that can serve as tools for further research. Texts from all disciplines relevant to the humanities are eligible for consideration.
Deadline: 1 July (for projects beginning 1 April of following year).
Inquiries: The Division of Research Grants
National Endowment for the Humanities
Mail Stop 350
806 15th St., N.W.
Washington, DC 20506
202-724-0226 Director and Deputy Director, Division of Research Grants
Preliminary inquiries, application forms, and *Program Announcement.*

104. *Name:*   *National Endowment for the Humanities* (NEH)
Division of Special Programs
Type: Science, Technology, and Human Values Program
Conditions: An area of continuing Endowment interest concerns the relationships among science, technology, and human values. In response to growing national concern about the value implications of new developments in science and technology, the National Endowment for the Humanities and the National Science Foundation jointly announced in 1973 a special interest in fostering research, education, and public-oriented activities in this subject. Proposals for projects in which the disciplines of the humanities will be predominantly employed may be submitted to the Endowment through one of its established divisional programs. For projects requiring major involvement of scientists, preliminary inquiry may also be made to the National Science Foundation, concerning the appropriateness of concurrent submission and review, with a view to possible joint funding by the two agencies. Endowment efforts in this area are coordinated through the Program of Science, Technology, and Human Values.

Inquiries: Office of Science, Technology and Human Values
National Endowment for the Humanities
Mail Stop 104
Washington, DC 20506
806 15th St., N.W.
202-724-0398 Director, Division of Special Programs
202-724-0354 Coordinator: Science, Technology, and
Human Values
Preliminary inquiries, application forms, and *Program
Announcement.*

105. *Name:* *National Endowment for the Humanities* (NEH)
Division of Special Programs, Office of Special Projects
Type: Grants
Conditions: The Office of Special Projects is the program in the Endowment responsible for supporting humanities projects
that do not fit precisely into any division's program, or
that fall between two divisions, or that are in totally
new areas of humanities activity. This program hopes to
be responsive to the best in the humanities for the broad-
est public without concern for the fact that a project
may or may not fit guidelines or may not be easily exe-
cuted. Special Projects tries in its funding to "widen the
area of the possible" and to strengthen the role of NEH
as a responsive, educational, public agency. Very often
a program that Special Projects initiates eventually becomes the basis for an expanded new program activity
within one of the regular divisions.
All applications to this program must be in the area of
the humanities as defined by the Endowment and should
present a fully outlined plan of operation and a detailed
budget. Initial inquiries should be in a brief 2–3 page
précis of the project. If the project is appropriate for
Special Projects, an application form will be returned.
Deadline: 1 March (for projects beginning 1 May).
1 June (for projects beginning in August).
1 September (for projects beginning 1 November).
1 December (for projects beginning in February).
Inquiries: Office of Special Projects
National Endowment for the Humanities
Mail Stop 303
806 15th St., N.W.
Washington, DC 20506
202-724-0398 Director, Division of Special Programs
202-724-0369 Program Officer, Special Projects
Preliminary inquiries, application forms, and *Program
Announcement.*

106. *Name:*   *National Endowment for the Humanities* (NEH)
Division of State Programs
    Type: Grants to support state and local humanities projects
    Conditions: The Division of State Programs makes grants to a citizens' committee created in each state in order to help support state and local humanities projects. The humanities committee in each state uses the funds awarded it by the Endowment to make grants, through open competition, in support of humanities projects designed by and responsive to the state's citizens. Each state humanities committee shapes its own program guidelines in the context of the state's resources and opportunities. Applicants submit proposals directly to their state humanities committee, according to that committee's guidelines.

The state humanities committees, collectively, make almost as many grants in the course of a year as does the Endowment itself. Projects supported by state committees frequently bring together scholars and the public in discussion of basic questions of human values, of history, and of cultural traditions. Special attention is given to projects designed to serve that portion of the public for whom access to and use of the humanities is limited. In this program the Endowment makes grants directly to the state committees only. Interested groups and organizations should write or call their state committee for further details about the committee's program. The addresses of all committees are listed in Appendix E.

    Deadline: 1 February (for projects beginning after 1 July).

1 May (for projects beginning after 1 October).

1 July (for projects beginning after 1 January).

1 November (for projects beginning after 1 April).

    Inquiries: Contact local committees.

202-724-0286 NEH Director, Deputy Director, and Individual Program Officers for the following five districts:

a. Donald Gibson for:

Alabama, California, Colorado, Kansas, Maine, New Hampshire, North Carolina, Oklahoma, Rhode Island, South Dakota, District of Columbia.

b. Gary Messinger for:

Alaska, Arkansas, Indiana, Maryland, Minnesota, Mississippi, Missouri, Nebraska, Ohio, South Carolina, Puerto Rico.

c. Julie Van Camp for:

Arizona, Florida, Georgia, Iowa, Kentucky, Massachusetts, Montana, New York, Pennsylvania, West Virginia, American Samoa.

d. Jim Vore for:

Connecticut, Michigan, Nevada, New Jersey, North

Dakota, Oregon, Tennessee, Vermont, Wisconsin, Wyoming, Virgin Islands.

e. Carole Watson for:
Delaware, Hawaii, Idaho, Illinois, Louisiana, New Mexico, Texas, Utah, Virginia, Washington, Guam.
Preliminary inquiries and *Program Announcement.*

107. *Name:*   *National Endowment for the Humanities* (NEH)
Office of Planning and Policy Assessment

Type: Grants

Conditions: In addition to supporting humanistic scholarship, education, and public-oriented activities, the Endowment is also interested in furthering evaluative and analytical work which will aid in understanding national needs in the humanities and in planning new or improved programs to meet such needs. Especially sought are proposals for the following:

a) Collection and analysis of data assessing the status and trends—including information about the financial, material, and human resources and significant or emerging problems—of important sectors of humanistic activity.

b) Design of models, techniques, and tools helpful in conducting policy research and analysis and in evaluating the effectiveness of institutional programs in the humanities.

c) Research, development, and demonstration of more efficient management and administrative methods for humanities organizations.

Deadline: Because of the limited funds available, only a small number of "Planning and Assessment Studies" can be supported each year. These projects are normally funded only after careful preparation and extensive consultation between staff, knowledgeable specialists in the field, and those proposing to undertake the study. Because of the nature of the projects supported and the developmental process through which most applications pass—first as an initial inquiry, and then as a preliminary proposal—there are no fixed deadlines. Potential applicants are advised to outline their study—with 2–3 pages usually sufficient to describe the study's purpose and need, general methodology, planned duration, and cost.

Inquiries: Program Officer
Planning and Assessment Studies, Office of Planning and Policy Assessment
National Endowment for the Humanities
Mail Stop 303
806 15th St., N.W.

Washington, DC 20506
202-724-0344

108. *Name:*   *National Humanities Center*
     Type: Fellowships
     Purpose: "To encourage advanced study in the humanities, to
                  bring humanistic scholars together with scholars in other
                  disciplines and with people in various fields of public
                  life, and to enhance the usefulness and influence of the
                  humanities in the United States."
     Number: 50 annually.
     Support: Stipends match normal academic incomes of the Fellows.
                  When Fellows have partial support in the form of sab-
                  batical salaries or other grants, the Center provides the
                  difference between that support and their normal salar-
                  ies. Travel expenses to and from the Center for Fellows
                  and their families. Secretarial services.
     Conditions: Fellows include both *scholars* of established reputation
                  and *young scholars* of promise who have held the *doc-
                  torate* less than nine years. Fellows also participate in
                  small seminars during the year. Applicants can be "hu-
                  manistically inclined scholars in the natural and social
                  sciences and the professions as well as scholars in fields
                  conventionally identified with the humanities."
     Duration: 1 year.
     Deadline: 10 January.
     Inquiries: National Humanities Center
                  Box 12256
                  Research Triangle Park, NC 27709
                  919-549-0661
                  Brochure and application forms.

109. *Name:*   *National Science Foundation*
     Type: Grants for research projects and in support of doctoral
                  dissertation research in linguistics
     Purpose: To support basic research.
     Deadline: Research proposals are reviewed three times yearly: in
                  fall, winter, and spring. Proposals must therefore be sub-
                  mitted at least 6 to 8 months prior to the start of the
                  project.
     Inquiries: Paul G. Chapin, Program Director for Linguistics
                  National Science Foundation
                  Washington, DC 20550
                  202-665-4000

110. *Name:*   *National Science Foundation*
     Type: NATO Postdoctoral Fellowships in Science
     Purpose: Support a broad range of scientific research, including
                  the history and philosophy of science.

Number:	About 40 annually.
Support:	$11,040 (for 12 months), plus travel and dependent allowance.
Conditions:	*U.S. citizens.* Candidates to have earned the *Ph.D.* Fellowships are tenable at nonprofit scientific institutions in foreign countries that are NATO members or which cooperate with NATO projects. Program designed primarily for *recent recipients of doctoral degree* (within past five years). Fellows may not simultaneously hold other grants or fellowships. Fellowships begin any time within one year after award announcement.
Duration:	6 to 12 months.
Inquiries:	National Science Foundation Division of Scientific Personal Improvement 1800 G St., N.W. Washington, DC 20550 202-282-7154 Announcement.

111.	*Name:*	*Newberry Library*
	Type:	Monticello College Foundation Fellowship for Women
	Purpose:	For research in residence at the Newberry by a woman scholar.
	Support:	$6,500.
	Conditions:	Applicants must be *women* who have the *Ph.D.* Award is designed for the younger woman whose career would be enhanced by the fellowship and who gives promise of scholarly productivity. Preference given to applicants whose research concentrates on the study of women, but any application appropriate to the collections of the Library (the humanities of western Europe from the late Middle Ages to modern times) will be considered. *N.B.* Funding of this award is uncertain. Write to Committee on Awards to inquire of its status.
	Duration:	6 months in residence at the Library.
	Deadline:	15 March.
	Inquiries:	Committee on Awards The Newberry Library 60 W. Walton St. Chicago, IL 60610 312-943-9090 Announcement.

112.	*Name:*	*Newberry Library*
	Type:	National Endowment for the Humanities Fellowships
	Purpose:	To encourage postdoctoral research and to increase opportunities for intellectual exchange through active participation in Library activities.
	Support:	Up to $18,000.

Conditions: Applicants must have the *Ph.D.* or its equivalent. Fellowship is designed for established scholars. Projects must be related to areas in which the Library has strong holdings (the humanities of western Europe from the late Middle Ages to modern times). Fellows are expected to participate in the life of the Newberry community. Fellowships are held in residence at the Library. Applicants may combine grants with sabbatical salary or other support.

Duration: 6 to 11 months.

Deadline: 1 February.

Inquiries: Committee on Awards
The Newberry Library
60 W. Walton St.
Chicago, IL 60610
312-943-9090
Announcement.

113. *Name:* *Newberry Library*

Type: Newberry-British Academy Fellowship for Study in Great Britain

Purpose: To allow established scholars to study in Great Britain in any field in which the Newberry collection is strong (the humanities of western Europe from the late Middle Ages to modern times).

Support: £ 8 per day.

Conditions: Fellowship is tenable in Great Britain. Applicants must be *scholars* whose field of specialty parallels some area in which the Newberry collection is strong (see above). Program gives preference to established scholars on the staffs of universities, museums, or libraries, especially to readers or staff of the Newberry. The Fellow's home institution is expected to pay salary during the term of the fellowship.

Duration: 3 months in Great Britain.

Deadline: 15 March.

Inquiries: Committee on Awards
The Newberry Library
60 W. Walton St.
Chicago, IL 60610
312-943-9090
Announcement.

114. *Name:* *Newberry Library*

Type: Short-term Resident Fellowship for Individual Research

Purpose: To underwrite revision for publication of a doctoral dissertation relating to the Library's holdings (the humanities of western Europe from the late Middle Ages to modern times).

Support: Stipends of up to $1000 for incidental expenses.
Conditions: Scholars must be without academic affiliation.
Duration: Up to 1 year.
Deadline: Applications may be submitted at any time.
Inquiries: Committee on Awards
                  The Newberry Library
                  60 W. Walton St.
                  Chicago, IL 60610
                  312-943-9090
                  Announcement.

115. *Name:*   *Newberry Library*
     Type: Short-Term Resident Fellowship for Individual Research
     Purpose: To support research in areas in which the Library has
                  strong holdings (the humanities of western Europe from
                  the late Middle Ages to modern times).
     Support: $500 per month (may be revised).
     Conditions: *Applicants,* who must normally reside more than 50 miles
                  from Chicago, will reside in Chicago during the fellow-
                  ship period. They must have the *Ph.D* or be *ABD*.
     Duration: 1 to 3 months.
     Deadline: 15 March for summer and fall fellowships.
                  1 November for winter and spring fellowships.
     Inquiries: Committee on Awards
                  The Newberry Library
                  60 W. Walton St.
                  Chicago, IL 60610
                  312-943-9090
                  Announcement.

116. *Name:*   *Office of Education*
                  Division of International Education
     Type: Faculty research abroad program in modern foreign
                  languages, area studies, and world affairs. Refer to:
                  Fulbright-Hays, section 102(b) (6).
     Purpose: To strengthen modern language and area studies cur-
                  ricula at American institutions.
     Conditions: *U.S. citizens.* Faculty members of U.S. institutions of
                  higher education. Fellowships are tenable in Egypt, India,
                  Pakistan, the Far East, Southeast Asia, East Europe, the
                  Soviet Union, the Near East, and Latin America.
     Duration: 3 to 12 months.
     Deadline: 1 November (anticipated).
     Inquiries: Faculty members should apply directly to their own
                  institutions.
                  Brochure available at:
                  Office of Education
                  Teacher Exchange Section, International Exchange
                  Branch

Division of International Education
Department of Health, Education, and Welfare
Washington, DC 20202
202-245-9692
N.B. Faculty research award program awards may be combined with grants from the International Research and Exchanges Board.

117. *Name:*   *Office of Education*
Division of International Education

Type: Summer Seminars abroad for educators. Refer to: Fulbright-Hays, section 102(b) (6).
Summer Seminar in Germany for Teachers of the German Language; Summer Seminar in Germany for College Teachers of German Studies; Summer Seminar in Italy for Teachers of the Classics; Summer Seminar in Italy for Teachers of the Italian Language; plus other Seminars projected for Brazil, Africa, and People's Republic of China.

Conditions: *U.S. citizens.* Two years' teaching experience. Present language teaching position on secondary or college level in any rank.

Duration: 1 Summer.
Deadline: 1 November (anticipated).
Inquiries: Office of Education
Teacher Exchange Section, International Exchange Branch
Division of International Education
Department of Health, Education, and Welfare
Washington, DC 20202
202-245-9692
Brochure and application form.

118. *Name:*   *Office of Education*
Division of International Education

Type: Teacher exchange program at foreign institutions
Conditions: *U.S. citizens.* Three years' teaching experience, present teaching position on elementary, secondary, or college level (up to assistant professor).

Duration: 1 year.
Deadline: 1 November; late opportunities sometimes available.
Inquiries: Office of Education
Teacher Exchange Section, International Exchange Branch
Division of International Education
Department of Health, Education, and Welfare
Washington, DC 20202

202-245-9700
Brochure and application form.

119. *Name:*   *The Carl and Lily Pforzheimer Foundation*
     Type: Grants
     Purpose: To assist scholars in carrying out projects of importance relating to the principal collections in the Carl H. Pforzheimer Library. (Principally, English and American literature, especially 19th century. Library is presently preparing *Shelley and His Circle.*)
     Number: Limited.
     Support: Varies.
     Deadline: Initial contact by letter required. Proposals due March, May, September, or November.
     Inquiries: Carl and Lily Pforzheimer Foundation, Inc.
70 Pine St., Rm. 3030
New York, NY 10005
212-442-5484

120. *Name:*   *Rockefeller Foundation*
     Type: a. Humanities Fellowships
              b. Humanities Fellowships in Human Rights
     Purpose: a. Humanities Fellowships: "To support the production of works of humanistic scholarship intended to illuminate and assess the value of contemporary civilization . . . Each fellowship proposal should seek to fulfill one or more of the following objectives: illuminate contemporary social, aesthetic, or cultural problems; search for comparative cultural values in a pluralistic world; explore the contemporary relevance of literary, artistic, cultural, historical, and philosophical traditions."
              b. Humanities Fellowships in Human Rights: To support research that seeks to clarify the concept of human rights. Research will be humanistic in nature and of broad contemporary relevance.
     Number: Humanities Fellowships: About 35 annually; Fellowships in Human Rights: About 6 annually.
     Support: Ordinarily $10,000 to $15,000. In most cases will not exceed $20,000. Grants may cover salary, benefits, travel, secretarial or research support, or research materials.
     Conditions: Applicants need not have an academic or institutional affiliation. Awards cannot be made for completion of graduate or professional studies, nor can proposal for the writing of poetry or fiction be considered. An applicant may not hold any other major fellowship concurrently, but may have concurrent sabbatical salary, or

small grants from other sources. Foreign citizens and subjects from abroad may apply, but applications must be in English. Fellowship holders must devote full time to their projects during tenure of fellowship.

Duration: Normally, 1 year. Awards will not be made for work occupying less than half a year or for projects limited to one or more summers.

Deadline: 1 October (for first stage proposals; second-stage proposals, when requested, by 17 December). Awards announced in March.

Inquiries: Rockefeller Foundation Humanities Fellowships or Rockefeller Foundation Humanities Fellowships in Human Rights:
The Rockefeller Foundation
1133 Ave. of the Americas
New York, NY 10036
212-869-8500
Brochure, *Rockefeller Foundation Humanities Fellowships,* lists several examples of research areas, names recipients and project titles of recent fellowships, and gives procedures for application.

121. *Name:*   *Rockefeller Foundation*
Type: Program for international conferences at the Bellagio Study and Conference Center, Lake Como, Italy
Purpose: To hold small conferences concerned with problems or topics of international significance.
Number: 40 to 45 throughout the year. Most conferences have between 20 and 25 participants, but the Center is also ideal for smaller working groups.
Support: At the Center, conferees are guests of the Foundation. (There are, however, no facilities for spouses or children of conferees.) The Foundation provides no monetary assistance to conferees, nor does it contribute toward travel expenses.
Duration: Approximately 1 week.
Conditions: Preference is given to conferences bearing some relationship to current program interests of the Foundation. Foundation interests in the humanities are:
a. Clarification of fundamental goals and values of contemporary society.
b. Humanistic efforts to provide an historical, philosophical, and cultural perspective on significant problems confronting contemporary society.
c. Preservation and revitalization of our American cultural heritage.
Deadline: There are no deadlines, but applications should be submitted as far in advance of the dates requested as pos-

sible. The Center closes yearly December 20 to January 20. Although there are no standardized forms, applications (in English) should contain:

  a. A full statement (2–10 pages) of the nature and purpose of the proposed conference.
  b. A tentative agenda.
  c. A list of probable participants, with the professional affiliations and nationalities of each.
  d. A statement of whether position papers will be prepared and available in advance to the Foundation as well as to the participants.
  e. The preferred dates for the conference, including several alternate dates.
  f. The institutional sponsorship of the conference.
  g. The names and full addresses of three persons, not connected with the proposed conference, who could provide a professional opinion as to the scope and value of the conference.
  h. A statement of how the travel costs of the participants are to be met.
  i. A statement of how the results of the conference will be published.

Inquiries: Susan Garfield, Coordinator
Bellagio Study and Conference Center
The Rockefeller Foundation
1133 Ave. of the Americas
New York, NY 10036
212-869-8500
Brochure.

122. *Name:* *Rockefeller Foundation*
   Type: Residential program for scholars at the Bellagio Study and Conference Center, Lake Como, Italy
   Purpose: To give scholars from around the world time to work on a significant project: a book, monograph, major article, musical composition, or other creative undertaking.
   Number: 80 to 90 throughout the year. Center accommodates 9 residents at a time; groups of 2 to 5 scholars working on related topics may be scheduled together.
   Support: At the Center, the resident and his/her spouse are guests of the Foundation. (There are, however, no facilities for children or for pets.) The Foundation provides no monetary assistance to residents, nor does it ordinarily contribute toward travel expenses.
   Duration: Approximately 4 weeks.
   Conditions: Many disciplines are represented, although projects addressing concerns of the Foundation receive preference. Foundation interests in the humanities are:

a. Clarification of fundamental goals and values of contemporary society.

b. Humanistic efforts to provide an historical, philosophical, and cultural perspective on significant problems confronting contemporary society.

c. Preservation and revitalization of our American cultural heritage.

Deadline: There are no deadlines, but applications should be submitted as far in advance of the dates requested as possible. The Center closes yearly December 20 to January 20. Although there are no standardized forms, applications (in English) should contain:

a. A detailed description of the project (5–10 pages).

b. If possible, a sample of previously published work related to the project.

c. A recent curriculum vitae.

d. A cover sheet which includes

   1. name, address, and affiliation

   2. name of spouse if he/she will accompany you

   3. preferred dates (including earliest and latest possible dates)

   4. title of project

   5. names and addresses of four referees whom Foundation might write for evaluation of your work

Inquiries: Susan Garfield, Coordinator
Bellagio Study and Conference Center
The Rockefeller Foundation
1133 Ave. of the Americas
New York, NY 10036
212-869-8500
Brochure.

---

123. *Name:*   *Smithsonian Institution*

    Type: Postdoctoral Visiting Research Fellowships

  Purpose: Postdoctoral research at the Institution in collaboration with a member of its staff. To further the research training of scholars and scientists in the early stages of their professional lives.

  Number: About 22 yearly.

  Support: $1,000 per month, plus research, and relocation allowances.

Conditions: Tenable at the Institution. Candidates must have recent *Ph.D.* (within 5 years) or its equivalent, "although the five-year limitation may be waived upon demonstration that a fellowship appointment would clearly be research training." Research fields are history of science and technology, history of art, American history, American material and folk culture, history of music and musical instruments, history of American and Oriental art, anthropology and linguistics, plus several scientific fields.

Duration: 6 to 12 months.
Deadline: 15 January.
Inquiries: Office of Fellowships and Grants
Smithsonian Institution
Washington, DC 20560
202-381-5855
Smithsonian Opportunities for Research and Study, revised edition available fall 1979.

124. *Name:* *Social Science Research Council* and *American Council of Learned Societies*
Type: Postdoctoral Grants for Research on Foreign Areas
Purpose: "To support research in one country, comparative research between countries in an area, and comparative research between areas." At present, program sponsors research by social scientists and by humanists in the following areas: Africa, contemporary and Republican China, the economy of China, Japan, Korea, Latin America and the Caribbean, the Near and Middle East since the beginning of Islam, South Asia, and Southeast Asia.
Support: $7,500 to $20,000, depending on the program.
Conditions: Generally, the *Ph.D.* or its equivalent. Grants are for "scholars whose competence for research in the social sciences or humanities has been demonstrated by their previous work." Grants may be used for travel, research expenses, or maintenance. Most programs require applicants to be *U.S.* or *Canadian citizens.*
Duration: 3 to 12 months, depending on the program.
Deadline: 1 December (announcement 1 April).
Inquiries: Social Science Research Council
Fellowships and Grants
605 Third Ave.
New York, NY 10016
212-577-9500
Brochure: *Fellowships and Grants.*

125. *Name:* *Social Sciences and Humanities Research Council of Canada*
Type: Grants for advanced research
Support: Varies; minimum of $2500 (Can.).
Conditions: *Canadian citizens* and those with one year's landed immigrant status in Canada. Faculty members can secure particulars through their campus representative.
Deadline: Any time for grants under $10,000 (announcements within 4 months); for grants over $10,000: 15 October,

Inquiries: 15 January, or 15 July (announcement within 6 months).
Social Sciences and Humanities Research Council of
Canada
255 Albert St., Box 1610
Ottawa, Ontario
Canada, KIP 6G4
613-995-9330
Brochure.

126. *Name:*   *Social Sciences and Humanities Research Council of
Canada*
Type: Leave fellowship
Purpose: To provide research time by supporting scholars on leave
of absence.
Support: $7,000 (Can.) for assistant professors, $9,000 (Can.)
for associate professors, $10,000 (Can.) for full profes-
sors. Plus travel allowance (in some cases), and up to
$2,500 (Can.) research costs.
Conditions: *Canadian citizen* and those with one year's landed immi-
grant status in Canada. *Ph.D.* Faculty members can se-
cure particulars through their campus representatives.
Duration: 6 to 12 months.
Deadline: 1 October.
Inquiries: Social Science and Humanities Research Council of
Canada
255 Albert St., Box 1610
Ottawa, Ontario
Canada, KIP 6G4
613-995-9330
Brochure.

127. *Name:*   *Social Sciences and Humanities Research Council of
Canada*
Type: Postdoctoral fellowships, program in aging
Purpose: To underwrite research by recent holders of the *Ph.D.*
in the field of aging.
Support: $18,000 (Can.), plus fringe benefits, and $2500 (Can.)
for research and travel expenses.
Conditions: *Canadian citizen.* Must have earned the *Ph.D.* within the
past three years.
Duration: 1 year; renewable for 1 year.
Deadline: 1 October (announcement in early January).
Inquiries: Social Sciences and Humanities Research Council of
Canada
255 Albert St., Box 1610
Ottawa, Ontario
Canada, KIP 6G4

613-995-9330
Brochure.

128. *Name:*   *Society of Fellows in the Humanities* (Columbia University)
Type: Postdoctoral fellowships in the humanities
Purpose: To allow recent Ph.D.s the opportunity for independent research and interdepartmental teaching.
Support: Stipend of $14,500; possibility of modest additional grants.
Conditions: Fellowship is held in residence at Columbia University. Fellows spend one-half of time in independent research, one-half time in interdepartmental teaching. Applicants must have received the *Ph.D.* within two-and-one-half years of the beginning of the fellowship (e.g., between 1 January 1978 and 1 July 1980 for a fellowship that begins in September 1980).
Duration: 1 academic year.
Deadline: 1 November.
Inquiries: Director
Society of Fellows in the Humanities
Room 1509, International Affairs Bldg.
Columbia University
New York, NY 10027
212-280-1754
Announcement and application forms.

129. *Name:*   *The Society for the Humanities* (Cornell University)
Type: Postdoctoral Junior Fellowships for Younger Scholars
Purpose: "To support and encourage creative research in the humanities, especially investigations that deal with essential humanistic concepts, stress the methods common to the several branches of the humanities, or explore the role that the humanities may have in the solution of urgent human problems."
Number: 5.
Support: $14,000 for the academic year.
Conditions: Applicants may be teachers and scholars in the humanities and arts, as well as professionals "who are articulate exponents of the humane significance of their professions." *Ph.D.* or its equivalent in exceptional cases. One or more years of college teaching experience. Fellowships are in residence at Cornell. Fellows conduct one informal weekly seminar each term. Society focuses on a theme each academic year (in 1980–81): "The relationship between Nature and Culture in the history of

civilization." Most of each Fellow's time is spent in study
or writing.

Duration: 1 academic year.

Deadline: 15 November for application and letters of recommendation. Announcement 10 February.

Inquiries: Professor Michael Kammen, Director
Society for the Humanities at Cornell University
Andrew D. White House
27 East Ave.
Ithaca, NY 14853
607-256-4086
Announcement, instructions, and application form.

130. *Name:* *Translations Center* (Columbia University)

Type: Language study fellowship

Purpose: To underwrite further language study abroad.

Support: $10,000.

Conditions: Applicant must have had previous study in the language for which fellowship application is made. Language study will be at an institution in the country where the language is spoken.

Number: 1 annually.

Duration: 1 year.

Deadline: 15 January.

Inquiries: Translations Center
Room 307A Mathematics Bldg.
Columbia University
New York, NY 10027
212-280-2305
Brochure and application form.

131. *Name:* *Translations Center* (Columbia University)

Type: Translations grants

Purpose: To support translations of literary works from lesser known languages into English.

Support: $500.

Conditions: Applicants must be qualified translators of lesser known languages. Grants are for translators of literary works. Grants limited to *U.S. citizens.*

Number: Varies; 7 in 1979.

Deadline: 15 February.

Inquiries: Translations Center
Room 307A Mathematics Bldg.
Columbia University
New York, NY 10027
212-280-2305
Brochure and application form.

132. *Name:* *United Chapters of Phi Beta Kappa*
  Type: Mary Isabel Sibley Fellowship
  Purpose: Research in Greek (language, literature, history, or archaeology) and French (language and literature).
  Number: 1 annually. Awarded alternately in each subject (French in 1980).
  Support: $7,000.
  Conditions: Unmarried *women,* between 25 and 35. Demonstrated ability for original research. If candidate has not completed Ph.D. must be *ABD.* Fellow must devote full-time work to research during fellowship year.
  Duration: 1 year.
  Deadline: 1 February.
  Inquiries: Mary Isabel Sibley Fellowship Committee
   United Chapters of Phi Beta Kappa
   1811 Q St., N.W.
   Washington, DC 20009
   202-265-3808
   Announcement.

133. *Name:* *University of Southern California*
  Type: Andrew W. Mellon Postdoctoral Fellowships in the Humanities
  Purpose: "To provide young humanists opportunities to develop a new area of research or to work in interdisciplinary teams in order to expand their capabilities or develop new areas of competence for their future career endeavors."
  Number: 3 annually.
  Support: Stipend of $14,000 for the academic year.
  Conditions: *Ph.D.* awarded within the past 7 years. Applicants may not hold tenure at an academic institution. Fellows will be appointed Visiting Assistant Professors in a department (English, German, or French and Italian). They will teach one course per semester, participate in on-going programs, pursue their own research, and participate in research activities of the Humanities Division about the year's theme or topic (1979–80 theme is the European Enlightenment).
  Duration: 1 year (not renewable).
  Deadline: 1 March.
  Inquiries: David H. Malone
   Dean, Division of Humanities
   University of Southern California
   Los Angeles, CA 90007
   213-741-2311
   Announcement.

134. *Name:*   *Villa I Tatti*
     Type: Fellowships
     Purpose: Research in all areas of Renaissance studies: history (including social, economic, scientific), history of art, history of music, philosophy, literature (Italian or neo-Latin), etc.
     Number: Approximately 7 annually.
     Support: Varies; up to $16,000 (most considerably less). I Tatti also offers a limited number of nonstipendary fellowships for scholars working in Florence on Renaissance subjects with support from other sources. Nonstipendary fellows should have the same qualifications and will have the same privileges as those whose stipends are derived from I Tatti funds.
     Conditions: Candidates should have the *Ph.D.* or its equivalent, be in the early stages of their careers and be working on a project requiring their presence in Florence or nearby centers.
     Duration: 1 July–30 June. Fellows are expected to be in Florence from September through June, except for brief trips.
     Deadline: 1 November.
     Inquiries: Send curriculum vitae, description of project, and three letters of recommendation to:
Director
Villa I Tatti
Via di Vincigliata, 26
50135 Florence, Italy

With a copy to:
Professor Walter Kaiser
401 Boylston Hall
Harvard University
Cambridge, MA 02138
617-878-7600
Announcement.

135. *Name:*   *Ludwig Vogelstein Foundation*
     Type: Grants
     Purpose: To provide support for projects involving creative work in the arts and unusual—particularly interdisciplinary—work in the humanities.
     Support: Up to $5000.
     Conditions: Preliminary letter required, containing outline of proposal, statement of funds requested, biographical details.
     Inquiries: Douglas Turnbaugh, Manager
Ludwig Vogelstein Foundation
Box 537
New York, NY 10033

136. *Name:*   *Woodrow Wilson International Center for Scholars*
                        Smithsonian Institution

    Type: Residential postdoctoral fellowship program

    Purpose: Postdoctoral research in social sciences, natural sciences, and humanities.

    Support: Center meets each Fellow's income for fellowship period (within limits).

    Conditions: *Ph.D.* Humanists are eligible to apply for admission to the Division of Historical and Cultural Studies (research in all humanities fields; welcomes proposals relating humanities to contemporary life), the Kennan Institute for Advanced Russian Studies (research on Russia and the U.S.S.R.), and the Latin American Program (research on Latin American and the Caribbean). Fellows devote full time to research and writing. The 1980 theme of the Center will be "Problems of Authority and Participation in Modern Society."

    Duration: 4 to 12 months.

    Deadline: 1 October.

    Inquiries: Wilson Center, Rm. 321
                        Smithsonian Institution Building
                        Washington, DC 20560
                        202-381-6247
                        Information and application materials.

B Deadlines

The following section has been arranged in two sections: those foundations with specific grant deadlines and those which will receive grant applications at any time. The number following each listing refers to the number assigned to each grant program in Appendix A. As part of the preliminary inquiries into programs of interest, the scholar should immediately inquire if the deadline date is the same as that in the following list. In the list, the following foundations are represented by acronyms:

> ACLS= American Council of Learned Societies
> IREX= International Research and Exchanges Board
> NEH= National Endowment for the Humanities

1 January	American Institute of Pakistan Studies, Villanova University: fellowships, 18
	Business and Professional Women's Foundation: BPW Foundation Research Grant programs; Lena Lake Forrest Fellowship, 28
	Institut Francais de Washington: Chinard Scholarships for research in France, 63
10 January	IREX: Slavonic studies seminar in Bulgaria, 71; summer exchange of language teachers with the USSR, 73
	National Humanities Center: fellowships, 108
11 January	Metropolitan Museum of Art, New York: Chester Dale Fellowship, 88; Mellon Fellowships, 89; J. Clawson Mills Scholarships, 91
15 January	Austrian Government Grants: Study, research, and travel, 26
	Gladys Krieble Delmas Foundation: fellowships for Venetian research, 41
	Kosciuszko Foundation: Scholarship and research grants for Polish studies, 79; 80
	Andrew Mellon Postdoctoral Felllowships, University of Pittsburgh: Postdoctoral fellowships, 86

25 March   William Andrews Clark Memorial Library UCLA: Mellon
                  Fellowship, 36
31 March   Dublin Institute for Advanced Studies: Scholarship to
                  School of Celtic Studies, 44
                  German Academic Exchange Service: Group information
                  visits, 50; short term research fellowships, 51; study
                  visits, 53
                  IFK-International Courses in German Language and
                  Philology: Scholarships for summer courses in Salzburg,
                  Austria, 61
                  IREX: Grants for Collaborative Activities and New Ex-
                  changes, 70; travel grants for senior scholars, 74
 1 April   NEH, Division of Fellowships: Grants for participants in
                  Summer Seminars for College Teachers, 94
15 April   Kate Neal Kinley Memorial Fellowship: Advanced study
                  of architecture, art, or music, 78
    May   Carl and Lily Pforzheimer Foundation: Grants, 119
 1 May   NEH, Division of State Programs: Grants to support state
                  and local humanities projects, for projects beginning
                  after 1 October, 106
15 May   NEH, Division of Research Grants: Research Publications
                  Program Grants, 98
31 May   IREX: Grants for Collaborative Activities and New Ex-
                  changes, 70; Travel Grants for Senior Scholars, 74
 1 June   Council for International Exchange of Scholars: Fulbright-
                  Hays Postdoctoral Awards—lecturing and research in
                  American Republics, Australia, and New Zealand, 39
                  NEH, Division of Fellowships: NEH Fellowships—Cate-
                  gories A and B, 93
                  NEH, Division of Special Programs: Special Projects
                  grants for projects beginning in August, 105
 1 July   ACLS: Travel grants for meetings abroad in November to
                  February, 14
                  Council for International Exchange of Scholars: Fulbright-
                  Hays Postdoctoral Awards—lecturing and research in
                  Asia, Africa, and Europe, 39
                  NEH, Division of Fellowships: Application for prospective
                  directors of Summer Seminars for College Teachers for
                  Seminars conducted the following summer, 94
                  NEH, Division of Research Grants, Research Materials
                  Program: Translation Grants for projects beginning 1
                  April, 103
                  NEH, Division of State Programs: Grants to support state
                  and local humanities projects for projects beginning
                  after 1 January, 106
15 July   Social Sciences and Humanities Research Council of Can-
                  ada: Research grants over $10,000, 125

31 July	German Academic Exchange Service: Group information visits, 50
September	Carl and Lily Pforzheimer Foundation: Grants, 119
1 September	College Art Association: Millard Meiss Publication Fund grants, 38
	NEH, Division of Special Programs: Special Projects grants for projects beginning 1 November, 105
15 September	NEH, Division of Research Grants, General Research Program: Basic Research Grants for projects beginning after 1 March, 99
	NEH, Division of Research Grants, General Research Program: State, Local, and Regional History Grants for projects beginning after 1 March, 100
30 September	ACLS: Fellowship program, 7
	ACLS: Research fellowships for recent recipients of Ph.D., 11
	IREX: Grants for Collaborative Activities and New Exchanges, 30; Travel Grants for Senior Scholars, 74
Fall	IFK-International Courses in German Language and Philology: Scholarships for summer courses in Salzburg, Austria, 61
October	NEH, Division of Fellowships: Summer Stipends, 95
1 October–15 October	American Institute of Indian Studies: Postdoctoral study tours of India, 15; Senior Research Fellowships in India, 16; travel grants to India, 17
1 October–31 December	Henry E. Huntington Library and Art Gallery: Research awards—NEH fellowships, 60
1 October	John Simon Guggenheim Memorial Foundation: U.S. and Canadian fellowships, 56
	NEH, Division of Research Grants, Research Materials Program: Editing Grants for projects beginning after 1 July, 101
	NEH, Division of Research Grants, Research Materials Program: Research Tools Grants for projects beginning after 1 July, 102
	Rockefeller Foundation: Humanities fellowships; humanities fellowships in human rights, 120
	Social Sciences and Humanities Research Council of Canada: Leave fellowships, 126; postdoctoral fellowships in aging, 127
	Woodrow Wilson International Center for Scholars, Smithsonian Institution: Postdoctoral humanities fellowships, 136
10 October	William Andrews Clark Memorial Library, UCLA: Mellon Fellowships, 36
15 October	Mary Ingraham Bunting Institute of Radcliffe College: Bunting Fellowships for women, 29; institutional nom-

Dumbarton Oaks Center for Byzantine Studies: Fellowships, 45

German Academic Exchange Service: Group information visits, 50

John Simon Guggenheim Memorial Foundation: Western hemisphere and Philippine Fellows Seeking further assistance, 56

31 December   Henry E. Huntington Library and Art Gallery: Research awards; NEH fellowships, 60

IREX: Grants for Collaborative Activities and New Exchanges, 70; Travel Grants for Senior Scholars, 74

C The Federal Information Centers

The Federal Information Center is a government agency with offices in most of the states and in the major cities throughout the United States. Its purpose is to provide information about the bewildering variety of federal agencies, services, and programs. Humanists interested in obtaining more specific information about the federal agencies listed in Appendix A can contact a local Federal Information Center. Furthermore, the centers can provide statistics or information that humanists might need in preparing grant or fellowship proposals. Below are listed the addresses and telephone numbers of local Federal Information Centers as of July 1979.

Alabama
Birmingham toll-free
  tieline to Atlanta,
  GA
322-8591
Mobile toll-free tieline
  to New Orleans, LA
438-1421

Arizona
Federal Building
230 N. First Ave.
Phoenix 85025
602-261-3313
Tucson toll-free tieline
  to Phoenix
622-1511

Arkansas
Little Rock toll-free
  tieline to Memphis,

TN
378-6177

California
Federal Building
300 N. Los Angeles St.
Los Angeles 90012
213-688-3800
Federal Building &
  U.S. Courthouse
650 Capitol Mall
Sacramento 95814
916-440-3344
Federal Building
880 Front St., rm. 1S11
San Diego 92188
714-293-6030
Federal Building &
  U.S. Courthouse
450 Golden Gate Ave.
Box 36082

San Francisco 94102
415-556-6600
San Jose toll-free tie-
  line to San Francisco
275-7422
Santa Ana toll-free tie-
  line to Los Angeles
836-2386

Colorado
Colorado Springs toll-
  free tieline to Denver
471-9491
Federal Building
1961 Stout St.
Denver 80294
303-837-3602
Pueblo toll-free tieline
  to Denver
544-9523

Connecticut

Hartford toll-free tie-
line to New York,
NY
527-2617

New Haven toll-free
tieline to New York,
NY
624-4720

District of Columbia

Seventh & D Sts., S.W.,
rm. 5716
Washington 20407
202-755-8660

Florida

Fort Lauderdale toll-
free tieline to Miami
522-8531

Jacksonville toll-free
tieline to St.
Petersburg
354-4756

Federal Building
51 S.W. First Ave.
Miami 33130
305-350-4155

Orlando toll-free tieline
to St. Petersburg
422-1800

William C. Cramer
Federal Building
144 First Ave. S.
St. Petersburg 33701
813-893-3495

Tampa toll-free tieline
to St. Petersburg
229-7911

West Palm Beach toll-
free tieline to Miami
833-7566

Georgia

Federal Building
275 Peachtree St., N.E.
Atlanta 30303
404-221-6891

Hawaii

Federal Building
300 Ala Moana Blvd.
Box 50091
Honolulu 96850
808-546-8620

Illinois

Everett McKinley
Dirksen Building
219 S. Dearborn,
rm. 250
Chicago 60604
312-353-4242

Indiana

Gary/Hammond toll-
free tieline to
Indianapolis
883-4110

Federal Building
575 N. Pennsylvania
Indianapolis 46204
317-269-7373

Iowa

Des Moines toll-free
tieline to Omaha,
NE
284-4448

Kansas

Topeka toll-free tieline
to Kansas City, MO
295-2866

Wichita toll-free tieline
to Kansas City, MO
263-6931

Kentucky

Federal Building
600 Federal Place
Louisville 40202
502-582-6261

Louisiana

U.S. Postal Service
Building

701 Loyola Ave.,
rm. 1210
New Orleans 70113
504-589-6696

Maryland

Federal Building
31 Hopkins Plaza
Baltimore 21201
301-962-4980

Massachusetts

J.F.K. Federal
Building
Cambridge St., 1st fl.
Boston 02203
617-223-7121

Michigan

McNamara Federal
Building
477 Michigan Ave.,
rm. 103
Detroit 48226
313-226-7016

Grand Rapids toll-free
tieline to Detroit
451-2628

Minnesota

Federal Building &
U.S. Courthouse
110 S. Fourth St.
Minneapolis 55401
612-725-2073

Missouri

Federal Building
601 E. 12th St.
Kansas City 64106
816-374-2466

St. Joseph toll-free tie-
line to Kansas City
233-8206

Federal Building
1520 Market St.
St. Louis 63103
314-425-4106

Nebraska
Federal Building
U.S. Post Office &
Courthouse
215 N. 17th St.
Omaha 68102
402-221-3353

New Jersey
Federal Building
970 Broad St.
Newark 07102
201-645-3600

Patterson/Passaic toll-
free tieline to
Newark
523-0717

Trenton toll-free tieline
to Newark
396-4400

New Mexico
Federal Building &
U.S. Courthouse
500 Gold Ave., S.W.
Albuquerque 87102
505-766-3091

Santa Fe toll-free tie-
line to Albuquerque
983-7743

New York
Albany toll-free tieline
to New York
463-4421

Federal Building
111 W. Huron St.
Buffalo 14202
716-846-4010

Federal Building
26 Federal Plaza,
rm. 1-114
New York 10007
212-264-4464

Rochester toll-free tie-
line to Buffalo
546-5075

Syracuse toll-free tie-
line to Buffalo
476-8545

North Carolina
Charlotte toll-free tie-
line to Atlanta, GA
376-3600

Ohio
Akron toll-free tieline
to Cleveland
375-5638

Federal Building
550 Main St.
Cincinnati 45202
513-684-2801

Federal Building
1240 E. Ninth St.,
rm. 137
Cleveland 44199
216-522-4040

Columbus toll-free tie-
line to Cincinnati
221-1014

Dayton toll-free tieline
to Cincinnati
223-7377

Toledo toll-free tieline
to Cleveland
241-3223

Oklahoma
U.S. Post Office &
Courthouse
201 N.W. 3rd St.
Oklahoma City 73102
405-231-4868

Tulsa toll-free tieline
to Oklahoma City
584-4193

Oregon
Federal Building
1220 S.W. Third Ave.,
rm. 109
Portland 97204
503-221-2222

Pennsylvania
Allentown/Bethlehem
toll-free tieline to
Philadelphia
821-7785

Federal Building
600 Arch St., rm. 1232
Philadelphia 19106
215-597-7042

Federal Building
1000 Liberty Ave.
Pittsburgh 15222
412-644-3456

Scranton toll-free tie-
line to Philadelphia
346-7081

Rhode Island
Providence toll-free tie-
line to Boston, MA
331-5565

Tennessee
Chattanooga toll-free
tieline to Memphis
265-8231

Clifford Davis Federal
Building
167 N. Main St.
Memphis 38103
901-521-3285

Nashville toll-free tie-
line to Memphis
242-5056

Texas
Austin toll-free tieline
to Houston
472-5494

Dallas toll-free tieline
to Forth Worth
749-2131

Fritz Garland Lanham
Federal Building
819 Taylor St.
Fort Worth 76102
817-334-3624

Federal Building &
U.S. Courthouse
515 Rusk Ave.
Houston 77002
713-226-5711

San Antonio toll-free
tieline to Houston
224-4471

Utah

Ogden toll-free tieline
   to Salt Lake City
399-1347

Federal Building
125 S. State St.,
   rm. 1205
Salt Lake City 84138
801-524-5353

Virginia

Newport News toll-free
   tieline to Norfolk

244-0480

Stanwick Building
3661 E. Virginia Beach
   Blvd., rm. 106
Norfolk 23502
804-441-6723

Richmond toll-free tie-
   line to Norfolk
643-4928

Roanoke toll-free tie-
   line to Norfolk
982-8591

Washington

Federal Building
915 Second Ave.
Seattle 98174
206-442-0570

Tacoma toll-free tieline
   to Seattle
383-5230

Wisconsin

Milwaukee toll-free tie-
   line to Chicago, IL
271-2273

D The Foundation Center

The Foundation Center is a nonprofit organization whose purpose is to provide information about the close to 30,000 American Foundations. The Foundation Center has organized a nationwide network of foundation reference collections for free public use. These collections fall within three basic categories. The four reference libraries operated by the Center offer the widest variety of user services and the most comprehensive collections of foundation materials, including all of the Center's publications; books, services and periodicals on foundations and philanthropy; and foundation annual reports, newsletters, and press clippings. The New York and Washington, D.C. libraries contain the IRS returns for all currently active private foundations in the United States. The San Francisco and Cleveland libraries contain the IRS records for those foundations in the western and midwestern United States respectively. The 76 cooperating collections generally contain IRS records for only those foundations within their state, although they may request information or copies of other records from the New York library.

Appendix A contains a list of those agencies whose main commitment has been to grants in the humanities and those whose grant-making is on a national scale. Because it would be impractical to do so, this list does not include every foundation that makes humanities grants. Specifically, foundations which only occasionally make humanities grants and foundations which limit their giving to one geographical area are not listed here. For those with energy and imagination, the resources of the national and the regional collections can be put to good use in identifying these smaller foundations and collecting the necessary information about them.

Reference collections operated by foundations or area associations of foundations are indicated by an asterisk. They are often able to offer special materials or provide extra services, such as seminars or orientations for users, because of their close relationship to the local philanthropic community. All other collections are operated by cooperating libraries. Generally, they are located within public institutions and are open to the public during a longer schedule of hours and also offer visitors access to a well-developed general library research collection. Please telephone individual libraries for more information about their holdings or hours. These addresses have been reprinted with the permission of The Foundation Center.

REFERENCE COLLECTIONS OPERATED BY THE FOUNDATION CENTER

The Foundation Center
888 Seventh Ave.
New York, NY 10019
212-975-1120

The Foundation Center
1001 Connecticut
Ave., N.W.

Washington, DC 20036
202-331-1400

The Foundation Center
Kent H. Smith Library
739 National City
Bank Building
Cleveland, OH 44114

216-861-1933

The Foundation Center
312 Sutter St.
San Francisco, CA
94108
415-397-0902

COOPERATING COLLECTIONS

Alabama

Birmingham Public
Library
2020 Park Place
Birmingham 35203
205-254-2541

Auburn University
at Montgomery
Library
Montgomery 36117
205-279-9110

Alaska

University of Alaska,
Anchorage Library
3211 Providence Dr.
Anchorage 99504
907-272-5522

Arizona

Tucson Public Library
Main Library
200 S. Sixth Ave.
Tucson 85701
602-791-4393

Arkansas

Westark Community
College Library

Grand at Waldron
Fort Smith 72913
501-785-4241

Little Rock Public
Library
Reference Department
700 Louisiana St.
Little Rock 72201
501-374-7546

California

Edward L. Doheny
Memorial Library
University of Southern
California
Los Angeles 90007
213-741-2540

San Diego Public
Library
820 E St.
San Diego 92101
714-236-5816

Colorado

Denver Public Library
Sociology Division
1357 Broadway
Denver 80203
303-573-5152

Connecticut

Hartford Public
Library
Reference Department
500 Main St.
Hartford 06103
203-525-9121

Delaware

Hugh Morris Library
University of Delaware
Newark 19711
302-738-2965

Florida

Jacksonville Public
Library
Business, Science, and
Industry Department
122 North Ocean St.
Jacksonville 32202
904-633-3926

Miami—Dade Public
Library
Florida Collection
One Biscayne Blvd.
Miami 33132
305-579-5001

Georgia
Atlanta Public Library
10 Pryor St., S.W.
Atlanta 30303
404-688-4636

Hawaii
Thomas Hale Hamilton
  Library
University of Hawaii
Humanities and Social
  Sciences Division
2550 The Mall
Honolulu 96822
808-948-8568

Idaho
Caldwell Public
  Library
1010 Dearborn St.
Caldwell 83605
208-459-3242

Illinois
Donors Forum of
  Chicago*
208 South LaSalle St.
Chicago 60604
312-726-4882
Sangamon State
  University Library
Shepherd Rd.
Springfield 62708
217-786-6633

Indiana
Indianapolis—Marion
  County Public
  Library
40 E. St. Clair St.
Indianapolis 46204
317-635-5662

Iowa
Public Library of Des
  Moines
100 Locust St.
Des Moines 50309
515-283-4259

Kansas
Topeka Public Library

Adult Services
  Department
1515 W. Tenth St.
Topeka 66604
913-233-2040

Kentucky
Louisville Free Public
  Library
Fourth and York Sts.
Louisville 40203
502-584-4154

Louisiana
New Orleans Public
  Library
Business and Science
  Division
219 Loyola Ave.
New Orleans 70140
504-586-4919

Maine
University of Southern
  Maine
Center for Research
  and Advanced Study
246 Deering Ave.
Portland 04102
207-780-4411

Maryland
Enoch Pratt Free
  Library
Social Science and
  History Dept.
400 Cathedral St.
Baltimore 21201
301-396-5320

Massachusetts
Associated Foundation
  of Greater Boston*
294 Washington St.,
  Suite 501
Boston 02108
617-426-2608
Boston Public Library
Copley Square
Boston 02117
617-536-5400

Michigan
Henry Ford Centennial
  Library
15301 Michigan Ave.
Dearborn 48126
313-271-1000
Purdy Library
Wayne State University
Detroit 48202
313-577-4040
Michigan State
  University Libraries
Reference Library
East Lansing 48824
517-353-8816
University of Michigan
  —Flint
UM—F Library
Reference Department
Flint 48503
313-762-3408
Grand Rapids Public
  Library
Sociology and
  Education Dept.
Library Plaza
Grand Rapids 49502
616-456-4411

Minnesota
Minneapolis Public
  Library
Sociology Department
300 Nicollet Mall
Minneapolis 55401
612-372-6555

Mississippi
Jackson Metropolitan
  Library
301 N. State St.
Jackson 39201
601-352-3677

Missouri
Clearinghouse for
  Midcontinent
  Foundations*
University of Missouri,

Kansas City
School of Education
Building
52nd St. & Holmes
Kansas City 64110
816-276-1176

Kansas City Public
Library
311 E. 12th St.
Kansas City 64106
816-221-2685

The Danforth
Foundation Library*
222 South Central Ave.
St. Louis 63105
314-862-6200

Springfield—Greene
County Library
397 E. Central St.
Springfield 65801
417-869-4621

Montana

Eastern Montana
College Library
Reference Department
Billings 59101
406-657-2320

Nebraska

W. Dale Clark Library
Social Sciences
Department
215 S. 15th St.
Omaha 68102
402-444-4822

Nevada

Clark County Library
1401 E. Flamingo Rd.
Las Vegas 89109
702-733-7810

Washoe County
Library
301 S. Center St.
Reno 89505
702-785-4190

New Hampshire

The New Hampshire

Charitable Fund*
1 South St.
Box 1335
Concord 03301
603-225-6641

New Jersey

New Jersey State
Library
Governmental
Reference
185 W. State St.
Box 1898
Trenton 08625
609-292-6220

New Mexico

New Mexico State
Library
300 Don Gaspar St.
Sante Fe 87501
505-827-2033

New York

New York State
Library
Cultural Education
Center
Humanities Section,
6th fl.
Empire State Plaza
Albany 12230
518-474-7645

Buffalo and Erie
County Public
Library
Lafayette Square
Buffalo 14203
716-856-7525

Levittown Public
Library
Reference Department
Building
1 Bluegrass Lane
Levittown 11756
516-731-5728

Rochester Public
Library
Business and Social
Sciences Division
115 South Ave.

Rochester 14604
716-428-7328

Onondaga County
Public Library
335 Montgomery St.
Syracuse 13202
315-473-4491

North Carolina

North Carolina State
Library
109 E. Jones St.
Raleigh 27611
919-733-3270

The Winston-Salem
Foundation*
229 First Union
National Bank
Building
Winston-Salem 27101
919-725-2382

North Dakota

The Library
North Dakota State
University
Fargo 58105
701-237-8876

Oklahoma

Oklahoma City
Community
Foundation*
1300 N. Broadway
Oklahoma City 73103
405-235-5621

Tulsa City-County
Library System
400 Civic Center
Tulsa 74103
918-581-5144

Oregon

Library Association of
Portland
Education and
Documents Room
801 S.W. Tenth Ave.
Portland 97205
503-223-7201

Pennsylvania

The Free Library of
Philadelphia
Logan Square
Philadelphia 19103
215-686-5423

Hillman Library
University of
Pittsburgh
Pittsburgh 15260
412-624-4528

Rhode Island

Providence Public
Library
Reference Department
150 Empire St.
Providence 02903
401-521-7722

South Carolina

South Carolina State
Library
Reader Services
Department
1500 Senate St.
Columbia 29211
803-758-3181

South Dakota

South Dakota State
Library
State Library Building
322 S. Fort St.
Pierre 57501
605-773-3131

Tennessee

Memphis Public
Library
1850 Peabody Ave.
Memphis 38104
901-528-2957

Texas

The Hogg Foundation
for Mental Health*
The University of
Texas
Austin 78712

512-471-5041

Dallas Public Library
History and Social
Sciences Division
1954 Commerce St.
Dallas 75201
214-748-9071

El Paso Community
Foundation*
El Paso National
Bank Building,
Suite 1616
El Paso 79901
915-533-4020

Funding Information
Library
Minnie Stevens Piper
Foundation*
201 North St. Mary's
St., Suite 100
San Antonio 78205
512-227-8119

Utah

Salt Lake City Library
Information and Adult
Services
209 E. Fifth St.
Salt Lake City 84111
801-363-5733

Vermont

State of Vermont
Department of
Libraries
Reference Services
Unit
111 State St.
Montpelier 05602
802-828-3261

Virginia

Richmond Public
Library
Business, Science, &
Technology
Department
101 E. Franklin St.
Richmond 23219
804-780-8223

Washington

Seattle Public Library
1000 Fourth Ave.
Seattle 98104
206-625-4881

Spokane Public Library
Reference Department
W. 906 Main Ave.
Spokane 99201
509-838-3361

West Virginia

Kanawha County
Public Library
123 Capitol St.
Charleston 25301
304-343-4646

Wisconsin

Marquette University
Memorial Library
1415 W. Wisconsin
Ave.
Milwaukee 53233
414-224-1515

Wyoming

Laramie County
Community College
Library
1400 E. College Dr.
Cheyenne 82001
307-634-5853

Puerto Rico

Consumer Education
and Service Center
Department of
Consumer Affairs
Minillas Central
Government
Building N.
Santurce 00908

Mexico

Biblioteca Benjamin
Franklin
Londres 16
Mexico City 6, D.F.

E State Humanities Committees

Committees fund local humanities projects under grants from the National Endowment for the Humanities. For a more complete description, including names and telephones of NEH program officers who deal with each state committee, see #106 in Appendix A.

Alabama

Alabama Committee for the
Humanities and Public Policy
Box 700, Birmingham Southern
College
Birmingham, AL 35204
205-324-1314

Alaska

Alaska Humanities Forum
429 D St., Rm. 211
Loussac Sogn Building
Anchorage, AK 99501
907-272-5341

Arizona

Arizona Humanities and Public
Policy Council
Suite 607, Arizona Bank Building
34 W. Monroe St.
Phoenix, AZ 85003
603-257-0335

Arkansas

Arkansas Humanities Program
University Tower Building
12th & University, Suite 1019

Little Rock, AR 72204
501-663-3451

California

California Council on the
Humanities in Public Policy
312 Sutter St., Suite 601
San Francisco, CA 94105
415-543-3865

Colorado

Colorado Humanities Program
855 Broadway
Boulder, CO 80302
303-442-7298

Connecticut

Connecticut Humanities Council
195 Church St.
Wesleyan Station
Middletown, CT 06457
203-347-6888, -3788

Delaware

Delaware Humanities Council
2600 Pennsylvania Ave.
Wilmington, DE 19806
302-738-8491

Florida

Florida Endowment for the
 Humanities
Let 360, University of South
 Florida
Tampa, FL 33620
813-974-4094

Georgia

Committee for the Humanities in
 Georgia
Georgia Center for Continuing
 Education
Athens, GA 30601
404-542-5481

Hawaii

Hawaii Committee for the
 Humanities
2615 S. King St., Suite 211
Honolulu, HI 96826
808-947-5891

Idaho

The Association for the Humanities
 in Idaho
Box 424
Boise, ID 83701
208-345-5346

Illinois

Illinois Humanities Council
201 W. Springfield Ave., Rm. 1002
Champaign, IL 61820
217-333-7611

Indiana

Indiana Committee for the
 Humanities
4200 Northwestern Ave.
Indianapolis, IN 46205
317-925-7195

Iowa

Iowa Board for Public Programs
 in the Humanities
Oakdale Campus
University of Iowa
Iowa City, IA 52242
319-353-6754

Kansas

Kansas Committee for the
 Humanities
112 W. Sixth St., Suite 509
Topeka, KS 66603
913-357-0359

Kentucky

Kentucky Humanities Council, Inc.
Ligon House
University of Kentucky
Lexington, KY 40506
606-258-5932

Louisiana

Louisiana Committee for the
 Humanities
Box 12, Loyola University
New Orleans, LA 70118
504-865-9404

Maine

Maine Council for the Humanities
 and Public Policy
Box 7202
Portland, ME 04112
207-773-5051

Maryland

The Maryland Committee for the
 Humanities and Public Policy
330 N. Charles St., Rm. 306
Baltimore, MD 21201
301-837-1938

Massachusetts

Massachusetts Foundation for the
 Humanities and Public Policy
237 E. Whitmore Administration
 Building
University of Massachusetts
Amherst, MA 01003
413-545-1936

Michigan

Michigan Council for the
 Humanities
Nisbet Building, Suite 30
Michigan State University
East Lansing, MI 48824
517-355-0160

Minnesota

Minnesota Humanities Commission
Metro Square, Suite 282
St. Paul, MN 55101
612-224-5739

Mississippi

Mississippi Committee for the
  Humanities
3825 Ridgewood Rd., Rm. 111
Jackson, MS 39211
601-982-6752

Missouri

Missouri State Committee for the
  Humanities, Inc.
6920 Millbrook Blvd.
St. Louis, MO 63130
314-889-5940

Montana

Montana Committee for the
  Humanities
Box 8036, Hellgate Station
Missoula, MT 59807
406-243-6022

Nebraska

Nebraska Committee for the
  Humanities
1915 W. 24th St., Rm. 216
Kearney, NE 68847
308-234-2110

Nevada

Nevada Humanities Committee
Box 8065
Reno, NV 89507
702-784-6587

New Hampshire

New Hampshire Council for the
  Humanities
112 S. State St.
Concord, NH 03301
603-224-4071

New Jersey

New Jersey Committee for the
  Humanities
Rutgers, The State University

CN 5062
New Brunswick, NJ 08903
201-932-7726

New Mexico

New Mexico Humanities Council
267 Geology Building
The University of New Mexico
Albuquerque, NM 87131
505-277-3705 (Albuquerque)
505-646-1945 (Las Cruces)

New York

New York Council for the
  Humanities
33 W. 42nd St.
New York, NY 10036
212-354-3040

North Carolina

North Carolina Humanities
  Committee
1209 W. Market St.
Greensboro, NC 27412
919-379-5325

North Dakota

North Dakota Committee for the
  Humanities and Public Issues
Patterson Hotel, Suite 500
Bismarck, ND 58501
701-258-9010

Ohio

Ohio Committee for Public
  Programs in the Humanities
760 Pleasant Ridge Ave.
Columbus, OH 43209
614-236-6879

Oklahoma

Oklahoma Humanities Committee
Executive Terrace Building
Suite 500, 2809 Northwest Expwy.
Oklahoma City, OK 73112
405-840-1721

Oregon

Oregon Committee for the
  Humanities
1633 S.W. Park

Portland, OR 97201
503-229-4821

Pennsylvania
Public Committee for the
  Humanities in Pennsylvania
401 N. Broad St.
Philadelphia, PA 19108
215-925-1005

Rhode Island
Rhode Island Committee for the
  Humanities
86 Weybosset St., Rm. 307
Providence, RI 02903
401-521-6150

South Carolina
South Carolina Committee for the
  Humanities
2801 Devine St.
McCrory Building
Columbia, SC 29205
803-799-1704

South Dakota
South Dakota Committee on the
  Humanities
University Station, Box 35
Brookings, SD 57006
605-688-4823

Tennessee
Tennessee Committee for the
  Humanities
Suite 202, Green Hills Office Park
1001 18th Ave. S.
Nashville, TN 37212
615-320-7001

Texas
Texas Committee for the
  Humanities and Public Policy
UTA Station, Box 19096
Arlington, TX 76019
817-273-3174

Utah
Utah Endowment for the
  Humanities in Public Safety

10 West Broadway
Broadway Building, Suite 200
Salt Lake City, UT 84101
801-531-7868

Vermont
Vermont Council on the
  Humanities in Public Policy
Grant House, Box 58
Hyde Park, VT 05655
802-888-5060

Virginia
Virginia Foundation for the
  Humanities and Public Policy
One B West Range
University of Virginia
Charlottesville, VA 22903
804-924-3296

Washington
Washington Commission for the
  Humanities, Inc.
Olympia, WA 98505
206-866-6510

West Virginia
Committee for Humanities and
  Public Policy in West Virginia
Box 204
Institute, WV 25112
304-768-8869

Wisconsin
Wisconsin Humanities Committee
716 Langdon St.
Madison, WI 53706
608-262-0706

Wyoming
Wyoming Council for the
  Humanities
Box 3274, University Station
Laramie, WY 82701
807-766-6496

Puerto Rico
Fundacion Puertorriquena de las
  Humanidades
Box 4307
Old San Juan, PR 00904
809-723-2087

Indexes

Index to Subjects in the Humanities

Many of the granting agencies listed in Appendix A do not limit their funding to research in a specific subject area of the humanities. The following numbers refer to those agencies with no subject restrictions that can be found in Appendix A: 5, 6, 7, 9, 11, 20, 26, 29, 31, 34, 43, 50, 51, 52, 53, 54, 56, 58, 63, 65, 84, 85, 86, 93, 95, 99, 105, 106, 108, 111, 112, 113, 114, 115, 120, 122, 125, 126, 128, 129, 133, 135, 136. There are programs, however, that do have restrictions. This subject index to individual areas in the humanities has been compiled for the scholar who has an interest in a particular area in the humanities. The number following each subject listed refers the user to the agency described in Appendix A as offering a grant for research or study in that subject.

Index to Places for Study

Many of the grants listed in Appendix A can be used for research or study anywhere in the world. The following numbers refer to those agencies with no geographic restrictions that can be found in Appendix A: 5, 6, 7, 8, 9, 11, 12, 13, 18, 20, 25, 27, 28, 34, 42, 43, 47, 56, 57, 59, 77, 78, 80, 87, 92, 93, 95, 99, 101, 102, 103, 104, 105, 109, 110, 120, 125, 126, 130, 131, 132, 135. However, some are limited. This geographic index has been compiled for the scholar interested in conducting research in a particular region. The number following each country or region listed refers the user back to the agency described in Appendix A as offering a grant for use in that area.